Affirmed

Discovering the Echoes of God's Truth Silenced by Life's Noise.

DO-votional

by

CHRYSTAL CASTILLO

AFFIRMED
Published by Watersprings Publishing, a division of
Watersprings Media House, LLC.
P.O. Box 1284
Olive Branch, MS 38654

© Copyrights 2019 Chrystal Castillo. All rights reserved.

No portion of this book may be reproduced, stored in a retrieval system or transmitted in any form or by any means (electronic, mechanical, photocopy, recording, scanning, or other), except for brief quotations in critical reviews of articles, without the prior written permission of the writer.

Scripture quotations marked "KJV" are taken from the King James Version.

Scripture quotations marked (NLT) are taken from the Holy Bible, New Living Translation, copyright © 1996. Used by permission of Tyndale House Publishers, Inc., Wheaton, IL 60189 USA. All rights reserved.

Printed in the United States of America.

Library of Congress Control Number: 2019903098

ISBN 13: 978-1-948877-11-4

*To my grandma Clara Blades, my number one fan.
To Donna Petagrew, the one who pointed me back to Christ
when I wanted to give up.*

Table of Contents

Introduction 7

AFFIRMATION 1: *I am Forgiven* 11
Chapter 1 - Religion 13
Chapter 2 - Bondage 19
Chapter 3 - Bitterness 26
Chapter 4 - Insecurity 31

AFFIRMATION 2: *I am Loved* 39
Chapter 5 - Hurt 40
Chapter 6 - Guilt 47
Chapter 7 - Shame 54
Chapter 8- Jealousy 61

AFFIRMATION 3: *I am Healed* 69
Chapter 9 -   Denial 70
Chapter 10 - Silence 76
Chapter 11 - Pride 83
Chapter 12 - Anger 90

AFFIRMATION 4: *I am Free* 97
Chapter 13 - Opinion 98
Chapter 14 - Fear 105
Chapter 15 - Lies 111
Chapter 16 - Idols 117

About the Author 122

Introduction

One morning my son had a doctors appointment to get a hearing test. We arrived at the doctor's office, checked in, and five minutes later my son's name was called. So, we headed back to the room with the tech. They had my son sit in this small room with speakers in every corner. In the front of the room was a huge window that allowed you to see into the room next door. The purpose of the test was to see if my son could hear a range of pitches. They can measure the quality of a child's hearing by rotating sound between each speaker and watching to see if the child looks toward the sound.

They placed my son in the middle of the room between two speakers. The Audiologist was in the room next door, but we could see her face through the huge window in the front of the room. My son was a bit distracted by the toys in the room, so it took a minute before they started the test. A few minutes later the Audiologist started making noise that came through the speakers. My son didn't look at the speaker, but he did hear the sound. He looked at the Audiologist through the window. He knew she was the source of the noise coming through the speaker.

There was a season in my life that I allowed the noise of my thoughts to be louder than the Word of God. I didn't realize where the noise was coming from so I gave it room to define who I was and what I was able to do. I learned in that season that God's Word affirms us. We don't have to continue to let the noise define us. God has a way of affirming, both through His word, and through our daily routine. I call these particular moments random revelations. He uses the most random things to speak to us.

I wrote this book because I want to empower you...yes, you that are currently reading this book. Look at the source of the noise that you hear in your daily thoughts and shatter it with the truth of God's Word. You know that noise that you hear whispering to you,

"Does God love me? "
"You can't handle this, just give up."
"No way, you can't give that up."
"Your past is who you are, why let it go?"

And the noise goes on. I am sure there is noise you hear right now in your life. Right now, as I am writing this I am hearing "Chrystal are you sure you want to publish this?" And very often I fail to look at the source of the noise that I hear. But we have a gift, the word of God. It is a tool of affirmation. It can change what we hear, but first, we must identify the source of the noise. If I don't know where it is coming from how can I shatter it?

I define noise as anything that we hear that is the very opposite of what God speaks in His Word. The source of the noise can be insecurity. I hear the noise "I am not good enough," but the source is my insecurity.

The truth is, that in the Word it says, "I am fearfully and wonderfully made."

In this book, I share my personal experiences that will help us identify the sources of the noise we hear. And guess what, we are going to speak back to that noise with the truth of God's word and shatter it together.

I call this book a *do-votional* because it's a little bit more than what you and I may typically call a devotional. Do-votionals are more than just encouraging words to read on a page. Do-votionals call for us to act. James 1:22 states that, "we ought to be doers of the word."

I have prayed for you. And I want to encourage and empower you. I look forward to walking on this journey with you.

Love,

Chrystal D. Castillo

"Now may the Lord of peace Himself give you His peace at all times and in every situation. The Lord be with you all."

2 Thessalonians 3:16 NLT

Instructions

How to use the sections in this book.

1. **The Noise:** We will identify the sound that conflicts with the Word of God in our lives.

2. **Defining the Source:** We will define what we hear in order to reconcile it with God's truth.

3. **The Truth that Echoes:** We will speak to the source of that noise with God's Word.

4. **The Discovery:** You will reflect inwardly and provide your personal thoughts and actions.

5. **The Affirmation:** You will shatter the source of the noise with affirmations that empower you and encourage you.

    You will *shout* these affirmations over all the *noise*:
    - ೲ I am Forgiven
    - ೲ I am Loved
    - ೲ I am Healed
    - ೲ I am Free

6. **Declaration:** You will speak to the noise and shatter its presence in your life.

7. **Memory Verse:** You will memorize these verses so you can hide the truth in your heart and enable it to echo when you hear life's noise.

    *Additionally, you will be asked to provide your own scriptures, affirmations or declarations. Look for this symbol: ▶

AFFIRMATION 1
I am Forgiven

1
Religion

The Noise

Religion is an aggressive sound. It gets louder when I mess up. As I look into the mirror before walking into the church, Religion says, "hello". "Mirror, mirror on the wall should I go to church? I messed up?"

Religion interrupts and says, "No you need to fix what you messed up before you go to church. You need to try to see if He will forgive you."

I decide not to go to church because I messed up BIG TIME, there's no way He will forgive me.

My favorite shirt had a huge stain on it. I decided to try to hand wash it. I would scrub and scrub, but the stain would not go away. I even tried to make up my own washing solution. Nothing that I did worked. I hated that I couldn't do anything to take away the stain. I had a pity party. It was my favorite shirt.

Religion makes me feel like I can get rid of my own stains. When I allow the sound of Religion to be louder than my relationship with God, I become frustrated. I try to play the role of savior and realize that there's nothing I can do to fix my mess. He forgives me, not because of what I do but because of who He is to me.

Sometimes we get so wrapped up in the religious practices that when we fall flat on our faces, we try to get back up by using things like our church attendance, tithing, as crutches to stand back up. Religion keeps us from declaring that we are forgiven because most of the time we think what we do is the source of our forgiveness.

He didn't choose us because we are perfect. He didn't die just so we can go to church, pay our tithes, etc. He died so that we may experience a relationship with Him. When He died, He didn't want us to become self-righteous, religious people. He died so that we could be free, forgiven people. When religion toots its horn, we should turn up the volume on our relationship with Jesus and shout I AM FORGIVEN. There's nothing we can do to win forgiveness, He has already given us the gift of grace. Today, will you accept this precious gift?

Defining the Source

Webster's dictionary defines Religion as a personal set, or institutionalized system of religious attitudes, beliefs, and practices. It is hard to accept that He has forgiven us when we believe our salvation hangs on the thread of our works. The Pharisees were religious. They were all about trying to prove what was right or wrong. They were all about works. Let's look at a story that will help us understand how the Pharisees operated.

And the scribes and Pharisees brought unto him a woman taken in adultery; and when they had set her in the midst.

John 8:3 KJV

Circle Pharisees. This word translates to the Greek word Pharisaios pronounced ä-rē-sī›-os meaning *exclusively religious.*

The primitive root of Pharisaios is the Hebrew word Parash pronounced pä·rash' meaning *to wound: —scatter, declare, distinctly, shew, sting.*

In John 8, we see that the Pharisees:

1. Brought a woman caught in the act of adultery (John 8:3)
2. Put her in front of the crowd of people (John 8:3)
3. Broadcasted her sin to the crowd (John 8:4)
4. Concluded that she needed to be stoned. They questioned Jesus (John 8:5)

They set out to humiliate her because according to them, her act of sin was unforgivable. They didn't think she was worthy of forgiveness. But Jesus responds in John 8:7 NLT,

They kept demanding an answer, so he stood up again and said, "All right, but let the one who has never sinned throw the first stone!"

Jesus put things in perspective for the Pharisees. None was deemed righteous, not even one. Our works are not currency for forgiveness. We couldn't say or do enough to earn salvation. It is by His blood, by grace that we can declare that we are forgiven.

In Acts 26 Paul tells his testimony. Part of his testimony had to do with him being religious.

> *If they would admit it, they know that I have been a member of the Pharisees, the strictest sect of our religion.*

Acts 26:5 NLT

Paul followed all the rules to the T. He lived as a Pharisee. He was very religious. He was a persecutor of the church. Things changed however in Acts 26:13-14 NLT.

> *About noon, Your Majesty, as I was on the road, a light from heaven brighter than the sun shone down on me and my companions. We all fell down, and I heard a voice saying to me in Aramaic, 'Saul, Saul, why are you persecuting me? It is useless for you to fight against my will.'*

Before he was Paul, he was Saul. God had a purpose for His life and decided to reveal Himself to Saul on the road of Damascus. Saul had zeal, but it was a waste. The conversion took place when he exchanged his life of religion for a relationship with Jesus Christ.

When we don't have a relationship with Christ it is hard to walk like we have been forgiven. Religion does not save us. Only a relationship with the REDEEMER will give us the security we need to declare that we are forgiven. Time to stop playing church. Before starting the next section, pray that God reveals to you the things that hinder you from confidently knowing that you are forgiven.

The Truth That Echoes

He said "IT IS FINISHED":
A jar of sour wine was sitting there, so they soaked a sponge in it, put it on a hyssop branch, and held it up to his lips. When Jesus had tasted it, he said, "It is finished!" Then he bowed his head and gave up his spirit.

John 19:29-30 NLT

Other Related Scripture(s):

He said "IT IS FINISHED" I know that everything that I will do now, and in the days to come is forgivable.

Revelation 16:17 NLT

His gift to me is salvation:
But there is a great difference between Adam's sin and God's gracious gift. For the sin of this one man, Adam, brought death to many. But even greater is God's wonderful grace and his gift of forgiveness to many through this other man, Jesus Christ.

Romans 5:15 NLT

Other Related Scripture(s): Romans 6:23 NLT, Ephesians 2:8-9 NLT

His gift to me is salvation, I didn't earn it, so I can't lose it.

HE PAID FOR MY SIN:
For you know that God paid a ransom to save you from the empty life you inherited from your ancestors. And it was not paid with mere gold or silver, which lose their value.

He paid for my sin, the forgiveness He grants me has nothing to do with my religious practices.

1 Peter 1:18 NLT

The Discovery

1. Have you accepted Him as Lord and Savior of your Life?
   _____
   _____
   _____

2. What questions do you have about your salvation? List the questions and begin to pray about the answers.
   _____
   _____
   _____

3. Right now, do you feel like you are forgiven? Why or why not?
   _____
   _____
   _____

4. Are you secure in your relationship with God? Why or why not?
   _____
   _____
   _____

5. If you were to die today do you know where you would spend eternity? Why?
   _____
   _____
   _____

6. Write out your testimony. How did you come to know Jesus?
   _____
   _____
   _____
   _____
   _____

Affirmed

The Affirmation

I AM FORGIVEN

His gift to me is salvation, I didn't earn it, so I can't lose it.

▶ _____

Declaration

I will no longer hide behind Religion because I have a relationship with God. I can say with boldness that I have been forgiven.

▶ _____

Memory Verse

"Oh, what joy for those whose disobedience is forgiven, whose sins are put out of sight. Yes, what joy for those whose record the Lord has cleared of sin."

Romans 4:6-8 NLT

2
Bondage

The Noise

Bondage captures me with its voice. The sound controls my every movement. I don't know how to silence it, so I continue to be manipulated by its words. I am overwhelmed. I feel trapped. The voice of the Lord is louder. I hear that I AM FORGIVEN. Just when I am convinced that I am forgiven Bondage comes and drags me away.

One day I put my oldest son in his car seat. I placed him in his chair and put the seatbelt over him. While driving I could hear him moving around in the back seat. I pulled over and looked at him. He had gotten out of his seat. He was no longer safe. I got out of the car and placed him back in his seat. I pulled the seatbelt back over him. When we arrived at our destination, I opened his door to get him out of the car. He tried to get out of the car but because he decided to move around some more the second time the seatbelt was wrapped around his legs. He couldn't get out. He was tangled.

When I allow the voice of Bondage to be louder than His forgiveness, I find myself tangled and not able to move forward. Bondage has a way of making me feel stuck when I have been forgiven. I don't have to be a pocket in the hands of my past. When Bondage becomes what I listen to I voluntarily surrender my truth of being forgiven.

You and I have been forgiven. We don't have to be slaves to our sin. He died for us, so we could walk in His forgiveness. Bondage only has a voice in our lives if we let it. The power of being forgiven is what silences bondage. We can declare with confidence that His cross is enough, and we are FORGIVEN.

Defining the Source

Webster's dictionary defines the word Bondage as: *A state of being bound usually by compulsion (as of law mastery) such as:*
A: captivity; serfdom
B: servitude or subjugation to a controlling person or force

I think we can agree that to be in bondage is to be in captivity. Let's look at the word Bondage in Romans 8:15 KJV,

> *For ye have not received the spirit of bondage again to fear;*
> *but ye have received the Spirit of adoption,*
> *whereby we cry, Abba, Father.*

Circle the word bondage. This word translates to the Greek word douleia pronounced du-la-a meaning *slavery*. The primitive root of this Greek word is douleuo pronounced du-lyu-o meaning *to be a slave to (literal or figurative, involuntary or voluntary- be in bondage (do) serve (ice).*

Look again at Roman 8:15 KJV above. I want you to notice something. When you see the word **spirit, <u>underline it</u>**. When it refers to bondage the word spirit is lowercase. When it refers to adoption the word Spirit is capitalized. When something is capitalized it means it has significance and typically means that we are referring to a person or place. Why do you think the word "spirit" was capitalized?

_____
_____
_____
_____
_____
_____
_____
_____

We see the same Greek translation of bondage in Galatians 5:1 KJV,

Stand fast therefore in the liberty wherewith Christ hath made us free, and be not entangled again with the yoke of bondage.

Highlight the word yoke. Before we look at the translation, what do you think of when you hear the word yoke?

_____

_____

_____

_____

_____

_____

_____

_____

_____

_____

The word yoke translates to the Greek word zygos pronounced zu-gos meaning from the root of zeugnymi (to join, especially by a "yoke); a coupling, i.e. (figuratively) servitude (a law or obligation); also (literally) the beam of the balance (as connecting the scales); - pair of balances yoke. A yoke is something that is tied to you. We see this idea in 2 Corinthians 6:14 when Paul instructs us to not be unequally yoked with unbelievers. To be yoked to someone means to be joined to someone. Bondage yokes (joins) us to things that are evil and unrighteous. These things can also be referred to as strongholds. 2 Corinthians 10:4 KJV,

For the weapons of our warfare are not carnal, but mighty through God to the pulling down of strong holds;

Circle the word strongholds. The word stronghold translates to the Greek word ochyrōma which is derived from the Greek word echo pronounced e'-kho meaning: *to hold (used in various application,* *literally or figuratively, direct or remote; such as possession; ability, continuity, relation, or condition.)*

Wow, that's how powerful a stronghold can be, it can take possession of your mind. It can literally hold you. The truth is we have been forgiven. His forgiveness is greater than our bondage, yoke or strongholds. We no longer have to be in bondage. His forgiveness has the power to break every chain/yoke and pull down every stronghold. As you prepare for the next section pray and ask God to reveal to you what has possession of your mind?

_____
_____
_____
_____
_____
_____
_____
_____
_____
_____
_____
_____
_____
_____
_____
_____
_____
_____
_____
_____

The Truth that Echoes

HE GRACIOUSLY FORGIVES ME

But there is a great difference between Adam's sin and God's gracious gift. For the sin of this one man, Adam, brought death to many. But even greater is God's wonderful grace and his gift of forgiveness to many through this other man, Jesus Christ.

Romans 5:15 NLT

Other Related Scripture(s): Luke 7:46-48 NLT, Find one more related scripture

▶ _____

His forgiveness is the reason why I gracefully ended my relationship with bondage.

HE ADOPTED ME

God decided in advance to adopt us into His own family by bringing us to Himself through Jesus Christ. This is what He wanted to do, and it gave Him great pleasure.

Ephesians 1:5

Other Related Scripture(s): Romans 8:15 NLT, Find one more related scripture

▶ _____

He adopted me, so I no longer have to be in bondage.

HE IS GREATER THAN ANYTHING

But you belong to God, my dear children. You have already won a victory over those people, because the Spirit who lives in you is greater than the spirit who lives in the world.

1 John 4:4 NLT

Other Related Scripture(s): Exodus 18:11 NLT, Find one more related scripture.

▶ _____

He is greater than any of my strongholds.

The Discovery

Below, write down your strongholds.
Example: Pleasing people

_____
_____
_____
_____

Why do you allow these things to have power over you?

_____
_____
_____
_____
_____
_____
_____
_____

What are you affirming within yourself to shatter the noise of Bondage?

_____
_____
_____
_____
_____
_____
_____
_____

The Affirmation

I AM FORGIVEN

His forgiveness has broken my chains of bondage.

 _____

Declaration

I am no longer a slave. I have been forgiven and adopted.

 _____

Memory Verse

We know that our old sinful selves were crucified with Christ so that sin might lose its power in our lives. We are no longer slaves to sin.

Romans 6:6 NLT

3
Bitterness

The Noise

Bitterness introduces itself and we shake hands. The sound of bitterness is so quiet, yet consuming. We grow closer and we bond. My heart kisses Bitterness and turns cold. I become chilled and numb. I don't like this feeling. I cannot accept that I have been forgiven because my heart is so numb that it's nonresponsive. He tells me "I am forgiven, and I have life" but the doors of my heart have been blocked with Bitterness.

One morning I took both of my boys into the kitchen for breakfast. My youngest son immediately demanded that I get him something and began to cry. I started cooking and getting things ready for them to eat. As I was preparing their plates, I noticed that he was still crying. He had gotten so upset that he couldn't even receive the plate that I had placed in front of him.

When my heart is filled with bitterness it's hard to accept God's forgiveness. His mercies are new every morning but when I allow bitterness to take over and speak, I am backed into a corner, placed in time out, and not free to enjoy the beauty of His forgiveness.

He died so that we can experience life. Part of accepting the life we have in Him is understanding that we have been forgiven. We can no longer allow bitterness to keep us from enjoying His forgiveness. We have been forgiven.

Defining the Source

Webster's dictionary defines bitterness as *marked by intensity or severity a: accompanied by severe pain and suffering. Bitterness in the New Testament is mentioned for the first time in Acts.*

For I perceive that thou art in the gall of bitterness, and in the bond of iniquity.

Acts 8:23 KJV

Put a circle around the word bitterness. This word translates to the Greek word pikria pronounced pe-kre-a meaning *acridity (especially poison), literally or figuratively: —bitterness.*

Bitterness can kill us if we are not careful. Has bitterness almost killed you internally? How? When?

_____

_____

_____

Read James 3:11-14. What are some of things that stand out to you in these verses?

_____

_____

_____

When we haven't fully accepted that God has forgiven us it keeps us from forgiving others. Not forgiving leads us to bitterness. Bitterness can lead us to hatred. Proverbs 10:12 KJV gives us a great illustration of what hatred can do:

Hatred stirreth up strifes; but love covereth all sins.

The word strifes translates to the Hebrew word medan pronounced med-an meaning discord, strife. Notice that love covers all sin. Love allows us to forgive. Love keeps us from growing bitter. If we say we have love in our hearts and we are bitter or hatful toward our brother or sister, can we truly declare that we have been forgiven? To be forgiven is to have the ability to forgive. Before starting the next section ask God if there is anyone that you need to forgive. Ask Him if there is any bitterness in your heart. Pray that He removes it so that you can enjoy His gift of forgiveness.

The Truth That Echoes

HE IS KIND:
He is so rich in kindness and grace that he purchased our freedom with the blood of his Son and forgave our sins.

Ephesians 1:7 NLT

Other Related Scripture(s): James 5:11 NLT, Romans 2:4 NLT

He is kind to me so that I may be kind to others.

He forgives me, so I can forgive others:

> *Make allowance for each other's faults, and forgive anyone who offends you. Remember, the Lord forgave you, so you must forgive others.*

Colossians 3:13 NLT

Other Related Scripture(s): Matthew 6:14 NLT, 2 Corinthians 2:10 NLT

He has forgiven me, not so I can be bitter, but be better and forgive those who offend me.

He came so that I may experience life abundantly:

> *The thief's purpose is to steal and kill and destroy. My purpose is to give them a rich and satisfying life.*

John 10:10 NLT

Other Related Scripture(s): Acts 17:25 NLT, John 4:14 NLT

He has given me life, so I don't have to sip the cup of bitterness.

The Discovery

In the past what has made you bitter?
Example: Losing a loved one

_____
_____
_____
_____

How easy is it for you to forgive someone?

_____
_____
_____
_____
_____
_____
_____

What are you affirming within yourself to shatter the noise of Bitterness?

_____
_____
_____
_____
_____
_____
_____
_____

The Affirmation

I AM FORGIVEN:
He has forgiven me so that I can forgive others. I am no longer bitter.

 _____

Declaration

I will no longer allow bitterness to poison my life I will pursue and enjoy this abundant life that He has gifted me with.

 _____

Memory Verse

We prove ourselves by our purity, our understanding, our patience, our kindness, by the Holy Spirit within us, and by our sincere love.

2 Corinthians 6:6 NLT

4
Insecurity

The Noise

Insecurity can be so noisy. Personally, it leaves me feeling like "I AM NOT FORGIVEN." I can quote scriptures all day, but insecurity can often silence the truth that I know. It greets me at the door of pity and leaves me hanging on empty. Within me lies shout out, "You are not worth it" "You don't deserve to be forgiven." When insecurity turns up its volume, I find myself stuck in my past. I have been at the point of tears wondering if He would forgive my past mistakes.

One morning I was walking down the stairs with our youngest son in my arms. While walking down the stairs it felt as though he was slipping from my arms. I was holding onto him with both arms because I didn't want him to fall. I never let go of him even though he let go of me. He started crying because he felt like he was going to fall. He was insecure in my embrace. Never once going down the stairs did I let go of him. I held him.

Insecurity gives me the perception that He has let go of me because of my sin. The minute I try walking forward in victory I find myself slipping and insecure in His embrace. I forget that He died so that I could live. He knew I would make mistakes before I arrived. He knew that I would let go of Him and chase after my fleshly desires and yet even in those moments, HE FORGIVES ME. He never lets go of me.

There are some days that we all look in the mirror and say to ourselves, "Why would He forgive me?", but when we open our Bibles and begin to read about how God views us, our perception changes. The word of God has the power to silence the noise of insecurity. When we read about how God views us that noise we hear becomes white noise. Insecurity is merely white noise trying to mask what God says about us. He says we are FORGIVEN.

Defining the Source

Webster's dictionary defines Insecurity as, the quality or state of not being firmly fixed in position. When I do a Bible search on the word insecurity there are no verses that come up. The word that I found to be pretty close to insecurity is unstable.

A double minded man is unstable in all his ways.

James 1:8 KJV

Circle the word *unstable* and underline the words *double and minded*. The word *unstable* in this verse translates to the Greek word Akatastatos pronounced ä-kä-tä›-stä-tos meaning *unstable, inconstant, restless.*

I had you to underline the words double and minded because I want us to look at what it means in the word of God. James 4:8 KJV is another place that we see the words double and minded:

Draw nigh to God, and he will draw nigh to you. Cleanse your hands, ye sinners; and purify your hearts, ye double minded.

Circle *double minded*. Double minded translates to the Greek word Dipsychos pronounced dē'-psü-khos meaning *two-spirited, i.e. vacillating (in opinion or purpose): —double minded.* So, we see that to be insecure, unstable, or double minded means that our mindsets and identity are wavering. The word wavering is also seen in James 1:6 KJV,

But let him ask in faith, nothing wavering. For he that wavereth is like a wave of the sea driven with the wind and tossed.

Circle *wavering* and highlight *wavereth*. Both words translate to the Greek word diakrinō pronounced dē-ä-krē'-nō meaning to *doubt, be partial, or stagger*. Let's look at the word stagger.

They grope in the dark without light, and he maketh them to stagger like a drunken man.

James 12:25 KJV

Circle *stagger*. This word translates to the Hebrew word Ta'ah pronounced tä·ä' meaning *to wander*.

Go back to the original definition of Insecurity and **circle firmly.** David paints a beautiful picture of what it means to be firmly planted.

And he shall be like a tree planted by the rivers of water, that bringeth forth his fruit in his season; his leaf also shall not wither; and whatsoever he doeth shall prosper.

Psalm 1:3 KJV

Circle the word planted. Go to the margin and draw a tree planted in water. In this verse the word planted translates to the Hebrew word Shathal pronounced shä·thal' literally **meaning** *to plant.*

Look at your drawing. A tree in water? Really? We just read about waves, winds and being tossed in James. But here we are planted, we are not moving. We cannot be moved because our roots are planted. Insecurity is basically a tree that someone planted on the surface of the ground just sitting and moving with the wind. When we are insecure our minds sit and move with whatever we hear.

Go back up to Psalm 1:3 and **underline the word *wither*.** The word *wither* translates to the Hebrew word Nabel pronounced nä·vāl' meaning *to wilt, to fall away, to be foolish, or lightly esteem.*

If a leaf on a tree withers, it loses its composure. Insecurity does that to us. Our composure changes therefore our posture changes. Our posture reflects what we speak over ourselves. Oh, we cannot be planted in the water if we speak that we are withering.

Psalm 1:1-2 KJV shows how we can keep from withering and how we get planted in the water:

Blessed is the man that walketh not in the counsel of the ungodly, nor standeth in the way of sinners, nor sitteth in the seat of the scornful. But his delight is in the law of the Lord; and in his law doth he meditate day and night.

Affirmed

- Who are you receiving counsel from?

- Are you reading His word?

Mediation of scripture is so important when it comes to changing our posture of insecurity. The Message Version puts Psalms 1:2 like this:

> *Instead you thrill to God's Word, you chew on Scripture day and night.*

What we chew is what we digest. Insecurity has a way of making us digest the very opposite of what the word of God says we are. Let's digest this today "I AM FORGIVEN, I HAVE THE MIND OF CHRIST. I AM SECURE IN HIM."

> *For, "who can know the LORD's thoughts? Who knows enough to teach him?" But we understand these things, for we have the mind of Christ.*

1 Corinthians 2:16 NLT

Since we have the mind of Christ, we can shatter the noise of insecurity. Pray and seek the Lord as you start the next section.

The Truth that Echoes

HE KNOWS ME:
You made all the delicate, inner parts of my body and knit me together in my mother's womb.

Psalm 139:13 NLT

Other Related Scripture(s): Jeremiah 1:5 NLT, Find one other related scripture

▶ _____

He knows everything about me, yet He forgives me.

I AM HIS:
But now, O Jacob, listen to the Lord who created you. O Israel, the one who formed you says, "Do not be afraid, for I have ransomed you. I have called you by name; you are mine.

Isaiah 43:1 NLT

Find two more related scriptures:

▶ _____
▶ _____

I am His, and my mistakes don't change how He views me.

HE HAS CHOSEN/CALLED ME:
We know, dear brothers and sisters, that God loves you and has chosen you to be his own people.

1 Thessalonians 1:4

Other Related Scripture(s): 1 Peter 5:10 NLT, Find one more related scripture:

▶ _____

He has chosen/called me, I do not have to be insecure in the assignments He gives me because I AM FORGIVEN.

The Discovery

Below write down the things that make you feel insecure about His forgiveness. Do you believe that He has forgiven you?

_____
_____
_____
_____
_____
_____
_____

What triggers your insecurity? What speaks the loudest?

_____
_____
_____
_____
_____
_____
_____

What are you affirming within yourself to shatter the noise?

_____
_____
_____
_____
_____
_____
_____

The Affirmation

I AM FORGIVEN
I am His, and He will never let go of me.

 _____

Declaration

I don't have to be insecure. I can walk confidently knowing that He has forgiven me.

 _____

Memory Verse

Thank you for making me so wonderfully complex! Your workmanship is marvelous—how well I know it.

Psalm 139:14 NLT

AFFIRMATION 2
I am Loved

5
Hurt

The Noise

Hurt is a voice that keeps me from hearing " I love you." It mutes the truth. Hurt interrupts a good relationship. It causes me to walk away from the very things that protect and challenge me. Hurt is so loud that it becomes a part of who I am. It is hard to know that I am loved when hurt gets involved. Hurt builds walls, creates chains, and then I find myself behind bars not able to move forward.

One day a lady called me out. I wanted her to comfort me. I wanted her to tell me what I wanted to hear. At that point, I didn't even know what I wanted to hear. This lady said what I needed to hear but because I view her words from a place of hurt, I walked away. I immediately cut off all fellowship with anyone outside of my home. I was hurt. I didn't want to have anything to do with anyone. The lady's words cut me deeply only because she didn't say what I wanted to hear. I didn't recognize that she was looking out for my best interest. I didn't see that she saw potential in me, and tried to challenge me, so I could grow. I didn't understand that her raising the bar and challenging me to reach it was her saying "Chrystal I love you too much to see you grow stagnant." I felt the opposite; I felt unloved.

In my relationship with the Lord, I have battled with His love. Not because I don't believe in Him, or believe Him, but because I have always identified His love with my circumstance. When I feel His comfort and things are going well, it's easy for me to know that He genuinely loves me. When He sits me down in venues that confront the things that need to be removed, within that is when I struggle to feel His love. I wrestle with it because punishment doesn't feel right. When I allow my hurt to speak over my circumstances, it keeps me from seeing that he loves me. Christ went through the greatest pain to demonstrate His love for us. He didn't do it so we could feel good. He didn't do it so we could be excluded from criticism or pain. He did it to confront our sin. There was not anything cute about His death. It hurt Him. He had real wounds. I am sure it didn't feel right, yet He did all so that His love for us can affirm us. His love has to speak over our hurt, not vice versa. When allowing His love to speak over our hurt, we can be affirmed and say with confidence " I AM LOVED BY HIM.

Defining the Source

Many factors contribute to the emotion of hurt. When I reflect on my personal experiences, I can see the common elements of betrayal or deception. For me, this occurred most often in the relationships that were dear to me. The word deceived translates to the Hebrew word Ramah pronounced rä·mä meaning to delude or betray'. We see this word illustrated in 1 Samuel 28:12 KJV.

And when the woman saw Samuel, she cried with a loud voice: and the woman spake to Saul, saying, Why hast thou deceived me? For thou art Saul.

Read 1 Samuel 28:8-12. Why did the woman feel deceived?

_____
_____
_____
_____

If we back up to the beginning of 1 Samuel 28, we see the word Romah. Look at 1 Samuel 28:3 KJV. **Circle the word Ramah.**

Now Samuel was dead, and all Israel had lamented him, and buried him in Ramah, even in his city. And Saul had put away those that had familiar spirits, and the wizards, out of the land.

I don't know about you, but deception and betrayal hurt. To be led on to believe something that is a lie. To be told a promise that never happens. I wanted to go this route because the word hurt in the Bible is mainly used to describe physical hurt and evil not necessarily the emotional hurt that we will speak of in this do-votional. In 80 of the verses in the King James Version Bible, the word hurt translates to the Hebrew word ra'a' pronounced rä·ah' meaning to do harm, evil, afflict, and punish. Isaiah 11:9 KJV,

> They shall not hurt nor destroy in all my holy mountain: for the earth shall be full of the knowledge of the LORD, as the waters cover over the sea.

Now let's see how Webster's Dictionary defines hurt:

1. A: To suffer pain or grief, B: To be in need
2. To cause damage or distress

At the beginning of this study, I used the words betrayal and deception to describe what may lead us to be hurt. We can also refer to hurt as affliction. When I think of affliction, I think of the story of Job. Look at Job 36:15 NASB

> He delivers the afflicted in their affliction,
> And opens their ear in time of oppression.

Circle the word afflicted above. This word translates to the Hebrew word 'aniy pronounced ä·nē' meaning depressed in mind or circumstance.

Highlight the word affliction above. Affliction translates to the Hebrew word 'oniy pronounced on·ē' meaning depression, misery.

Our hurt can also be described as affliction. We can go through a challenging season that leaves us in what I like to call the "wilderness." Job lost everything. Even though he had a relationship with God, it was a very dark season for him.

Lastly, sometimes we are hurt because of a death of a loved one. We experience great grief. It is so painful to go through losing the people we love. I have been hurt because of family members leaving this earth (in my opinion) too soon. You can get over betrayal/deception, get through a time of affliction but grief is a whole other level of hurt. My husband and I had lost our baby not too long ago, and it is one of the hardest things that I have ever had to walk through. In the book of Ruth Naomi experiences the death of her sons. Read Ruth 1 to understand the story a little better.

Would ye tarry for them till they were grown? would ye stay for them from having husbands? nay, my daughters, for it grieveth me much for your sakes that the hand of the Lord is gone out against me.

Ruth 1:13 KJV

Circle the word grieveth above. This word translates to Marar pronounced mä·rar' meaning to be bitter. To be moved by choler.

Grief can lead us to be bitter. I don't know where you are at in life right now but if you are experiencing hurt in any of these ways:

1. Betrayal/Deception/Offense

2. Affliction/Tribulation

3. Death of a loved one

I want you to know that God loves you. He sent us His Son also known as the High Priest. I love this verse in Hebrews 4:15 NLT,

This High Priest of ours understands our weaknesses, for He faced all of the same tests we do, yet He did not sin.

We can go to God with our hurt because He understands, and He is so faithful to comfort us. Pray and prepare your heart for the next section.

The Truth that Echoes

HE CORRECTS ME:
And have you forgotten the encouraging words God spoke to you as his children? He said,

"My child, don't make light of the LORD's discipline, and don't give up when he corrects you. For the LORD disciplines those he loves, and he punishes each one he accepts as his child."

Hebrews 12:5-6 NLT

Other Related Scripture(s): Deuteronomy 8:5 NLT, Revelation 3:19 NLT

He corrects me because He loves me. When I am hurting, I can rest and know that He has my best interest in mind.

HE PROTECTS ME:
For you bless the godly; O LORD; you surround them with your shield of love.

Psalm 5:12 NLT

Other Related Scripture(s): Proverbs 2:8 NLT, Psalm 23:4 NLT

He protects because He loves me. Sometimes my hurt is the result of my own decisions. He protects me by redirecting me. If I chose to still walk towards the things, He is protecting me from I will get hurt.

HIS LOVE WILL NEVER FAIL ME:
Praise the Lord! He is good. God's love never fails. Praise the God of all gods. God's love never fails.

Psalm 136:1-2 NLT

Other Related Scripture(s): Jeremiah 31:3 NLT, Find one more related scripture

▶ _____

His love will never fail, I can be secure even in times when I am experiencing my greatest hurt. People may fail, the plans that I have may fail, but His love for me will never fail. His love goes beyond my hurt. His love is greater than my feelings.

The Discovery

Pray and ask God to reveal any hurt you have. What did He reveal to you?

___

Is the hurt that He revealed to you keeping you from believing that you are loved by God?

___

Do you believe that your relationship with God would be different if that hurt were removed?

___

Are you ready to let it go?

___

Affirmed

The Affirmation

I AM LOVED:

His love will never fail me.

Declare

The almighty God loves me. My hurt is not greater than His love for me.

Scripture Memory

For the Lord, your God is living among you. He is a mighty savior. With his love, he will calm all your fears. He will rejoice over you with joyful songs.

Zephaniah 3:17 NLT

6
Guilt

The Noise

Guilt is an overwhelming echo that recites my past elegantly, like a poet. Line after line. I am in the audience listening, and I find myself dancing with the band playing behind the echo. As I stand, I say, "Yeah that's me." Love taps me on my shoulder and asks if I want to get away from the noise playing. I am so in tune with the poet I say no. I'd rather sit and listen then to leave with love. What sounded oh so fun to listen to turns into sounds of war. Suddenly I find myself sitting in the audience of my battle. I then realize that love never left. The echo was so loud that I couldn't see that love was sitting next to me.

I was so hurt by the lady that pulled me aside that I decided to walk away from that community. I didn't like what she had to say because it brought up issues that I needed to face. Months after leaving I felt myself feeling guilty. My actions were wrong. I started attending a new church. I went through a season of drought. I was spiritually dead because my guilt was beating me up. My sin put me in the corner. I was trapped. I started thinking about the relationship I had with the lady and what would happen if I would ever see her again. Would she embrace me? I was wrong. How could she ever want to speak to me again?

Anytime I mess up I find myself avoiding prayer. I walk away from communicating with the Lord because my guilt reminds me that I was wrong. I feel so guilty at times that I feel as though He wouldn't want to speak to me. When I allow guilt to lead me, I miss the fact that God has His arms open ready to receive me. Though I am imperfect, I AM LOVED BY HIM.

While we were deep in our sin, He chose us. He knew we were

going to mess up, so He sent His Son. Not just for yesterday's mistakes, but tomorrow, and the next day and so forth. We can be affirmed even when we mess up because He pursued us. Our imperfection cannot separate us from His love. Nothing can ever separate us from His love. His love never fails, and it never gives up on us. Even we mess up we can shout "I AM LOVED."

Defining the Source

Let's do a little background on the history of sin before we break down the word GUILT. In the Old Testament sacrifices had to be made for sins to be forgiven. People would do burnt offerings and sacrifice things of value for many different reasons, but one of the main reasons was for their sins to be pardoned. The word sacrifice translates to the Hebrew word zabach pronounced zä·vakh' meaning *to offer, kill, slay*.

Look and study the passages below. Please make a note of why the sacrifice was being made:

- Genesis 46:1-3
- Exodus 20:23-25

We will come back to the word sacrifice and tie everything together. Let's look at the story of Isaiah when he saw the Lord: Look up Isaiah 6:5 KJV and read it.

The word "woe" here translates to the Hebrew word owy meaning *passionate cry of grief or despair.*

Why did the conversation start with "woe is me"? (Isaiah 6:5a)

In the second part of Isaiah 6:5 Isaiah lists reasons why he was grieved or in despair. List them:

Now let's look at the word GUILT. Webster defines guilt as:

1. The state of one who has committed an offense especially consciously
2. Feelings of deserving blame especially for imagined offenses or from a sense of inadequacy

I believe Isaiah felt grieved and in despair because he was guilty of sin. In the Old Testament the word guilty translates to the Hebrew word Rasha' pronounced rä·shä' meaning guilty one, one guilty of a crime.

Here is the word in Numbers 35:31 KJV,

Moreover ye shall take no satisfaction for the life of a murderer, which is guilty of death: but he shall be surely put to death.

In the New Testament the word guilty translates to the Greek word enochos pronounced en'-okh-os meaning *held in, bound by, liable to (a condition, penalty or imputation).*

Let's read the NASB version of Matthew 5:21,

"You have heard that [a]the ancients were told, 'YOU SHALL NOT COMMIT MURDER' and 'Whoever commits murder shall be [b]liable to the court.

When you are guilty, you are liable. In Matthew 5:21, if you murder someone, you break the law. Therefore, you are guilty. In the Old Testament sacrifices (zabach) were made as payments for sin. A wage was needed to pay for our wrongdoing. Here's where it all ties in, you and I were guilty, but The Greatest sacrifice was made, so we no longer have to pay for our guilt. I love how it paints this idea in the book of Hebrews.

Read Hebrews 7:27 NLT. Unlike those other high priests, he does not need to offer sacrifices every day. They did this for their own sins first and then for the sins of the people. But Jesus did this once for all when he offered himself as the sacrifice for the people's sins.

And he did not enter heaven to offer himself again and again, like the high priest here on earth who enters the Most Holy Place year after year with the blood of an animal. If that had been necessary, Christ would have had to die again and again, ever since the world began. But now, once for all time, he has appeared at the end of the age[a] to remove sin by his own death as a sacrifice.

Hebrews 9:25-27 NLT

Highlight "once for all time." So, Christ's death satisfies our death sentence. We deserve death. We are guilty, but He sacrificed His life so that we could have fellowship with the Father that created us. That's some love right there. Now that we have unpacked and defined the word, spend time in prayer before you begin the next section.

The Truth that Echoes

HIS LOVE FREES ME FROM GUILT:
And the results of God's gracious gift are very different from the result of that one man's sin. For Adam's sin led to condemnation, but God's gift lead to our being made right with God, even though we are guilty of many sins.

Romans 5:16 NLT

Other Related Scripture(s): 1 Corinthians 15:17 NLT, Find one more related scripture

 _____

I know that He loves me because He endured the Cross, so I would not have to remain guilty.

HE LOVED ME WHEN I WAS GUILTY:
But God is so rich in mercy, and he loved us so much that even though we were dead because of our sins, he gave us life when he raised Christ from the dead (It is only by God's grace that you been saved.)

Ephesians 2:4-5 NLT

He loved me when I was deep in sin, so I can now rest and know that I am loved by Him. He continues to forgive me when I mess up:

When people work, their wages are not a gift, but something that they have earned. But people are counted as righteous not because of their work, but because of their faith in God who forgives sinners.

Romans 4:4-5 NLT

Other Related Scripture(s): 1 John 1:9 NLT, Find one more related scripture

▶ _____

He loves and forgives me.

The Discovery

We all feel guilty about something. It can be the smallest thing that makes us feel guilty. What guilt are you carrying around?

_____
_____
_____
_____
_____
_____
_____
_____

How does your guilt affect your relationship with God?

_____
_____
_____
_____
_____
_____
_____
_____

Are you ready to let it go? Why or why not?

_____

The Affirmation

I AM LOVED:

His love freed me from guilt.

 _____

Declaration

I don't have to avoid being in His presence due to my short-comings. I can go to Him boldly because I am loved by Him.

 _____

Memory Verse

Under the old covenant, the priest stands and ministers before the altar day after day, offering the same sacrifices again and again, which can never take away sins. But our High Priest offered himself to God as a single sacrifice for sins, good for all time. Then he sat down in the place of honor at God's right hand.

Hebrews 10:11-12 NLT

1
Shame

The Noise

Shame is a soft whisper that comes like a gentle breeze. As I sit, I watch that breeze blow everything that is in front of me away. I can't even enjoy the sweet blessings of love because of shame. As soon as I begin to embrace what I have received, shame blows it away. Shame makes me feel unworthy of love. It's annoying because I desire to have to experience love, but shame hides me from the greatest love that there is His love.

On Wednesday night I find myself trying to park in the place that I left. I left this place because I was hurt and didn't want to return because I felt guilty. As soon as I walked out of my vehicle, I saw that lady greeting people at the door. While walking up to the door, I was thinking, what will she say when she sees me. I was getting ready to walk in, and she grabbed and hugged me. She acknowledged me amid me trying to hide. I didn't expect her to embrace me. I didn't think I deserved her hug. It was in that moment that I experienced love.

There are so many times that I feel unworthy of His love. My shame lies to me, making me believe that I don't deserve to be loved. Shame keeps me from being in His arms. I find it hard to worship when I feel shame. I stay in my seat and listen to the music. I miss out on experiencing His love when I allow shame to dictate what I am worthy of receiving. He called me by name and marked me as His own. He loved me beyond my worth. I AM LOVED.

The love He has for us goes deeper than what we could ever comprehend. He loves us, we don't have to hide from Him. Let's take off our cover of shame and run to His arms. Come out of your hiding place and let Him see your face. Let Him tell you that " He loves you." You don't have to cover up who you are or what you have done. Today declare I AM LOVED.

Defining the Source

We can start with the Webster Dictionary definition of Shame:

1. A painful emotion caused by consciousness of guilt, shortcoming, or impropriety
2. A condition of humiliating disgrace or disrepute
3. Something that brings censure or reproach;

We previously defined guilt so if you want to go back and refer to "guilt "you can. For the sake of this do-votional, we will go with the second definition. The story of Adam and Eve is a classic when it comes to describing shame.

And Adam said, this is now bone of my bones, and flesh of my flesh: she shall be called Woman because she was taken out of Man. Therefore, shall a man leave his father and his mother, and shall cleave unto his wife: and they shall be one flesh. And they were both naked, the man and his wife, and were not ashamed.

Genesis 2:23-25 KJV

Circle "not ashamed." Ashamed in this particular passage translates to the Hebrew word buwsh pronounced bush meaning shamed or confounded.

In this case, they were not humiliated. They didn't do anything wrong. They were husband and wife, so they didn't have to be shameful. God gives Adam a command in Genesis 2:16-17 KJV:

And the Lord God commanded the man, saying, Of every tree of the garden thou mayest freely eat: But of the tree of the knowledge of good and evil, thou shalt not eat of it: for in the day that thou eatest thereof thou shalt surely die.

Eve gets tempted in Genesis 3, and of course if you know the story you know that she eats from the tree and convinces Adam to eat the fruit. If you don't know the whole story read Genesis chapter 3. After they eat the fruit Genesis 3:7 NLT says:

*At that moment their eyes were opened, and they suddenly felt **shame** at their nakedness. So they sewed fig leaves together to cover themselves.*

Genesis 3:8 KJV, this perfect couple that didn't have anything to be ashamed of hears God's voice and starts hiding:

And they heard the voice of the Lord God walking in the garden in the cool of the day: and Adam and his wife hid themselves from the presence of the Lord God amongst the trees of the garden.

They hid because they were ashamed of what they did. Of course God already knew, look at the rest of the story

Genesis 3:9-11 KJV

And the Lord God called unto Adam, and said unto him, Where art thou? And he said, I heard thy voice in the garden, and I was afraid, because I was naked; and I hid myself. And he said, Who told thee that thou wast naked? Hast thou eaten of the tree, whereof I commanded thee that thou shouldest not eat?

Circle the word hid. The word hid translates to the Hebrew word chaba' pronounced khä·vä' meaning *to secrete, hide (self), do secretly.*

So they went from Genesis 2:25 to hiding in Genesis 3:10. They were hiding because they did something wrong.

We read about sacrifices in the guilt do-votional. If you study more of the Old Testament you will learn that the people of God would have to hear from God through the prophets. Jesus changed that whole dynamic. We now know that Jesus came and died so we can be freed from our guilt. If He freed us from sin and the guilt that birthed from our sin, why do we feel shame? Why hide from the presence of the Lord when we have been forgiven and freed? Look at this verse:

God has united you with Christ Jesus. For our benefit God made him to be wisdom itself. Christ made us right with God; he made us pure and holy and he freed us from sin.

1 Corinthians 1:30 NLT

Affirmed

The word "freed" is "redemption in the KJV. It translates to the Greek word apolytrōsis pronounced ä-po-lü'-trō-sēs meaning *ransom in full.*

RANSOM IN FULL: now that's love. He died because He wanted us to have a relationship with Him. We can go to the throne of grace.

Let us therefore come boldly unto the throne of grace, that we may obtain mercy, and find grace to help in time of need.

Hebrews 4:16 KJV

He wanted to bring heaven to earth so we could experience His love. We don't have to feel shamed like Adam and Eve. We can come into His presence and ask for forgiveness and draw near to Him. You and I are loved by THE KING of KINGs and Lord of Lords. He nailed shame on the cross. Pray and ask Him to free you of your shame so you can be in His presence during your time of reading.

The Truth that Echoes

HE GAVE ME A NEW LIFE AND MADE ALL THINGS NEW:

He died for everyone so that those who receive his new life will no longer live for themselves. Instead, they will live for Christ, who died and was raised for them. So, we have stopped evaluating others from a human point of view. At one time we thought of Christ merely from a human point of view. How differently we know him now. This means that anyone who belongs to Christ has become a new person. The old life is gone; a new life has begun!

2 Corinthians 5:15-17 NLT

Other Related Scripture(s): Romans 4:17 NLT, Colossians 2:12 NLT

He has given me a new life and made all things new, I don't have to be ashamed of my past. What I did, or will do, does not disqualify me from being in His presence. He loves me. He knows me and calls me His own:

But now, O Jacob, listen to the Lord who created you. O Israel, the one

who formed you says, "Do not be afraid, for I have ransomed you. I have called you by name; you are mine.

Isaiah 43:1 NLT

Other Related Scripture(s): John 10:14 NLT, Matthew 10:29-31 NLT

He knows me and calls me His own I can rest in His love. I don't have to be afraid of approaching Him.

I can be in His presence:

Yet now he has reconciled you to himself through the death of Christ in his physical body. As a result, he has brought you into his own presence, and you are holy and blameless as you stand before him without a single fault.

Colossians 1:22 NLT

Other Related Scripture(s): Jude 1:24 NLT, Find one more related scripture

▶ _____

He loves me so much that I can come in His presence without shame. I don't have to hide. I can boldly approach the throne of grace.

The Discovery

Pray and ask God to reveal any shame. What did He reveal to you?

_____
_____
_____
_____
_____
_____

Is the shame that He revealed to you keeping you from believing that you are loved by God?

_____
_____
_____
_____
_____
_____
_____

Do you believe that your relationship with God would be different if that shame was removed?

_____
_____
_____

The Affirmation

I AM LOVED:
He gave me a new life and made all things new

▶ _____

Declaration

I will not be afraid to be in His presence.

▶ _____

Memory Verse

*May I be blameless in keeping your decrees;
then I will never be ashamed.*

Psalm 119:80 NLT

8
Jealousy

The Noise

Anger and Jealousy are sisters. They like to gang up on me. Anger bullies me and Jealousy rings. I ignore the call. Voicemails are downloaded reminding me of what I don't have. I call and instead of answering, Jealousy shows up when the woman that has everything I want stands in front of me smiling. Even though I have the option of deleting the voicemails, I replay them over and over again. I think to myself "Why did He give her the things that I deserve? What's so special about her? How could He love me and not give me the same things as her?" His love speaks, but in that moment, I refuse to listen because I am caught up in what someone else has. I know that He loves me but seeing others with what I want makes me question His love for me.

    My two boys enjoy eating food. I love seeing them run to the table. Even though my youngest cannot climb into his seat, he always stands and waits for me to pick him up. My oldest climbs into his chair and begins waiting for a plate to arrive. With both boys finally in their seats, I start prepping their food. My oldest likes to tap his hands on the table while he waits. If it takes too long, my youngest throws a fit. He starts screaming. After I finish cooking their food I serve them their plates. My oldest gobbles down his food. His plate is empty, so he looks at me and his eyes say MORE. He then looks over at his brother's plate and gets upset. In his mind, he feels like he is missing out. I give them the portions that they need. I know not to give my oldest more than what he can digest because he can get greedy. I know not to give my youngest too much because he will end up wasting his food. They lack no good thing because I know the amount that they need.

    In moments of jealousy, I begin to reflect on what I don't have and start denying that He loves me. I allow what I don't or do have to define His love. I am guilty of not seeing that the husband he gave me, the children he allowed me to have, and everything I have are reflections of His love for me. He loves me so much that He knows exactly what I need and supplies it. The portions He gives me cannot be compared to other portions because He intentionally, lovingly gave it to me.

When we answer the call of jealousy, it is easy to get distracted by what God is doing in other people's lives. We serve a good God. He is The Great Shepherd, and He gives all of us exactly what we need. daily bread. We must learn to be content in the space He has us in. Hang up that call. Look around at all that you have and there you will find His love. You are loved.

Defining the Source

I want you to draw a tree in the margin. Draw three roots, and we will name each one. Go ahead and draw leaves on the tree. The leaves will represent jealousy. Our three roots are perspective, comparison, and possessiveness.

Perspective is probably the biggest root out of the three. Webster's dictionary defines perspective as:

1. A mental view or prospect.
2. The appearance to the eye of objects in respect to their relative distance and position.

In the Bible, we don't see the actual word "perspective," but there are several verses with the word "think." The way we think is reproduced from our perspective. Philippians 4:8 KJV,

Finally, brethren whatsoever things are true, whatsoever things are honest, whatsoever things are just, whatsoever things are pure, whatsoever things are lovely, whatsoever things are of good report, if there be any virtue, and if there be any praise, think on these things.

Circle the word think above. In this verse, the word "think" translates to the Greek word Logizomai pronounced lo-gē'-zo-mī meaning *to take inventory, conclude and reason.*

To have a perspective that doesn't birth jealousy, we must take inventory of the thoughts we have daily. We must conclude good things. Often our perspective produces jealousy in us because in our minds we magnify what someone else may have and sometimes it leads us to question if God loves the same way He loves that person.

Onto our next root. When we have a poor perspective, we sometimes can find ourselves comparing our lives to other people's lives. Honestly, I have compared my gifts to others. I find myself saying " I wish I could..." and those small little sayings turn into jealousy. We see the word compare in Isaiah 40:18 KJV,

> To whom then will ye liken God? or what likeness will ye compare unto him?

In this verse the word "Compare" translates to the Hebrew word 'Arak pronounced 'a-rak' meaning *to arrange, set in row, put in order.*

This is exactly what we do when we compare ourselves to others. Mentally we line up everything we have ever accomplished and set it to a row of someone else's accomplishments. This only leaves us jealous or arrogant. 2 Corinthians 10:12 KJV,

> For we dare not make ourselves of the number, or compare ourselves with some that commend themselves; but they measuring themselves by themselves, and comparing themselves among themselves, are not wise.

The word compare in this verse translates to the Greek word sygkrinō pronounced sün-krē'-nō meaning *to judge one thing in connection with another.*

Typically when we do this we don't have the proper view. So you may look at the fact that someone else just got a new car and you are stuck with your old car that barely works. You feel like you got the short end of the stick. You see the new car but you don't see that she is going through a terrible divorce. Jealousy blurs reality. Jealously grows when we feast off of comparrison.

Lastly, posseiveness is another root of jealousy. When we want to protect what is ours. When we feel like what we have has the possibility of being taken away. We assume that someone or something is a threat to what we have so we get jealous. I can give an example. In college I met my best friend. I really didn't know what it meant to have a best friend, I just knew that we connected and we were cool. We pretty much did everything together. We washed clothes in the dorm, we ate lunch in the Cafeteria, and even took some classes together. While that same year we became best friends she met a new group of people. We stop hanging out as much as we usually did so jealousy begin to take place within me. I thought the people were a threat to our friendship, again I didn't know what it meant to be a good friend back then.

The word jealous in the Bible describes a trait of God. Really, God being jealous ? NO WAY. Let's look at this word within the context of scripture.

For thou shalt worship no other god: for the Lord, whose name is Jealous, is a jealous God: Lest thou make a covenant with the inhabitants of the land, and they go a whoring after their gods, and do sacrifice unto their gods, and one call thee, and thou eat of his sacrifice;

Exodus 34:14 KJV

Let's look at this in the New Living Translation Version so that we can get a clear understanding of what these verses are speaking to us.

You must worship no other gods, for the Lord, whose very name is Jealous, is a God who is jealous about his relationship with you. You must not make a treaty of any kind with the people living in the land. They lust after their gods, offering sacrifices to them. They will invite you to join them in their sacrificial meals, and you will go with them.

Exodus 34:14 NLT

Now go back to the KJV and **circle the word jealous.** The word jealous in this verse translates to the Hebrew word Qanna' pronounced kan·nä' which comes from the Hebrew word Qana' pronounced kä·nä' meaning *zealous, i.e. (in a bad sense) jealous or envious.*

In other words God wants us to make Him number one. The difference between the jealousy He has, and what we have is righteousness. He pursues us and protects us because we are precious to Him. We are possessive in our protection of others or things. According to Webster's dictionary *passiveness* means that we are:

1. Not willing to share things with or lend things to other people:

2. Wanting all of someone's attention and love

Webster's dictionary defines jealousy as:

1. Hostile towards rival or one believed to enjoy an advantage

2. Intolerant of rivalry or unfaithfulness

3. Vigilant in guarding possession.

All three of these definitions tie into the roots that we have covered. In Christ we are all family and we are called to be kind to one another. Instead of leaves of jealousy sprouting from our tree we want to produce fruits of the spirit mentioned in Galatians 5:22-23 NLT,

> But the Holy Spirit produces this kind of fruit in our lives: love, joy, peace, patience, kindness, goodness, faithfulness, gentleness, and self-control. There is no law against these things!

In order to produce the fruits of the spirit our roots must be planted in the spirit and not our flesh.

> Those who belong to Christ Jesus have nailed the passions and desires of their sinful nature to his cross and crucified them there. Since we are living by the Spirit, let us follow the Spirit's leading in every part of our lives. Let us not become conceited, or provoke one another, or be jealous of one another.
>
> **Galatians 5:24-26 NLT**

Let's draw another tree in the margin that is planted in the spirit. Write out the fruits of the spirits over the top of the tree. Now pray before you begin the next section.

The Truth that Echoes

HE IS MY SHEPHERD:

Now may the God of peace— who brought up from the dead our Lord Jesus, the great Shepherd of the sheep, and ratified an eternal covenant with his blood—may he equip you with all you need for doing his will. May he produce in you, through the power of Jesus Christ, every good thing that is pleasing to him. All glory to him forever and ever! Amen.

Hebrews 13:20-21 NLT

Other Related Scripture(s): Psalm 23:1

Find one more related scripture
▶ _____

He is my shepherd. He tends to me because He loves me, and I have all that I need.

HE IS MY INHERITANCE:

Lord, you alone are my inheritance, my cup of blessing. You guard all that is mine.

Psalm 16:5 NLT

Other Related Scripture(s): Lamentation 3:24 NLT

Find one more related scripture
▶ _____

He is my inheritance all that I need is in Him. He is everything!!!

HE IS GOOD:

The Lord is good to everyone. He showers compassion on all his creation.

Psalm 145:9 NLT

Other Related Scripture(s): 1 Chronicles 16:34 NLT, Find one more related scripture
▶ _____

He is good, everything I have is good and is a reflection of His love for me.

The Discovery

Below write down the things that you think you should have. What do you feel like you lack in your life?
Example: Marriage, Children, Health

_____
_____
_____

1. If He never gave you any of these things, would you think that He doesn't love you?

   _____
   _____
   _____
   _____
   _____
   _____
   _____
   _____

2. What are you affirming within yourself to shatter the noise of Jealousy?

   _____
   _____
   _____

Affirmation

I AM LOVED:
He is my shepherd; I have all that I need.

 _____

Declaration

I don't have to be jealous of anyone. He loves me and "I LACK NO GOOD THING."

 _____

Memory Verse

*Taste and see that the Lord is good.
Oh, the joys of those who take refuge in him!*

Psalm 34:8 NLT

Affirmed

AFFIRMATION 3
I am Healed

9
Denial

The Noise

Denial has a charming voice. When it speaks, I listen. It woos and convinces me that Truth is no good. Denial flirts with me, and I am flattered. Truth comes along and asks me on a date. I am stuck on denial that I turn away from Truth. Denial smiles, and seconds later we find ourselves at the beginning of a lustful courtship. Truth stays and waits. I don't want to hear Truth's voice because it's not appealing to me at the moment. When I am in a relationship with Denial, I miss the opportunity to walk with Truth. When I refuse to walk with Truth, it becomes tough for me to know Him as a HEALER.

For a while, my husband and I walked around offended every time someone would recommend for us to get our son tested for Autism. We would question their judgment. It was clear that our son needed to be evaluated, but instead of facing reality we decided to walk around like everything was all good. One day we saw him around a group of typical children, and it was then that we realized that we were walking in denial. He could have gotten help and resources at an earlier age, but because of our denial, the process of him developing functioning skills was prolonged.

When I am in denial and rightfully know that I am, I fail to realize that God can only heal what is true. He cannot heal what my feelings decide to believe or a made-up condition. Walking in the truth allows me to believe that He can heal my broken heart, my past, and my health conditions. In announcing my reality, I get the rich discovery of His healing power.

You and I don't have to walk in denial. We don't have to fear the truth. It's hard believing that your ex-boyfriend broke your heart, that your past left scars, and that you may have some health issues, but HE IS A HEALER. Be affirmed, and know that when you pick truth over denial, YOU can indeed be HEALED.

Defining the Source

Webster's dictionary defines denial as the *refusal to admit the truth or reality of something*. Wow, the refusal to admit the truth. It's not the fact that we don't know the truth it's that we refuse to acknowledge it. We see a clear example of denial when Simon Peter betrays Jesus:

And Simon Peter stood and warmed himself.
They said therefore unto him, Art not thou also one of his disciples? He denied it, and said, I am not.

John 18:25 KJV

So, Simon Peter knows that he is a disciple of Jesus and refuses to admit the truth. **Circle the word denied**. This word translates to the Greek word arneomai pronounced är-ne'-o-mī meaning to *contradict*. The root of är-ne'-o-mī is another Greek word rheō pronounced rhe'-ō meaning *to utter, speak or say, command, make*.

When we deny what we speak it becomes what we believe to be true. The truth always shows its face. When we try to deny that we are sick we say with our mouths that we don't need healing. When we deny our truth, we also deny the fact that we can be healed and restored. We think because we reject our reality that it will eventually just go away. We don't like to sit in what is uncomfortable. We would love to run and deny what God can use to show us that He is HEALER. In Mark 9 we read about a father that is desperately in need of a miracle for his son. I love how the father admits that he doesn't fully believe, Mark 9:24 NLT:

The father instantly cried out, "I do believe, but help me overcome my unbelief!"

Instead of admitting our unbelief we sit in denial. We are blinded by our mindsets and paralyzed by our own understanding of God. Our denial has a way of putting God in a box. He is God. The One that lived before the universe. The One who lived outside of time, yet we limit Him. Self-denial has to take place before we can experience Him. He wants us to know Him as HEALER and RESTORER. We see this idea of self-denial in the Word over and over again. Here goes a popular verse

> *Then said Jesus unto the disciples, if any man will come after me, let him deny himself, and take up his cross, and follow me.*
>
> **Matthew 16:24 KJV**

Circle the word deny. This word translates to the Greek word Aparneomai meaning *to disown*.

Webster's dictionary defines disown as: *To refuse to acknowledge as one's own*

1. To repudiate any connection or identification with
2. To deny the validity or authority of

The problem is we detach from the wrong things. We love to own the blessings that He gives us but refuse to own the sickness and/or hardship. We disown the very things that God uses to bring Him the most glory. We must come to the end of ourselves to find Him. We can deny our pain and miss Him, or we can deny ourselves, take up our realities and let Him lead us on a journey of healing. He wants to invite us to know Him as HEALER. Please pray about the things you deny either in speech or deed before you start the next section.

The Truth that Echoes

HE IS A HEALER:
*O Lord my God, I cried to you for help,
and you restored my health.*

Psalm 30:2 NLT.

Other Related Scripture(s): Psalm 103:3 NLT, Psalm 147:3NLT, Isaiah 57:18-19 NLT

He is a HEALER I don't have to hide or deny my reality. He is more than able to heal me.

HE HAS A PLAN FOR MY LIFE:
*For I know the plans I have for you," says the Lord.
"They are plans for good and not for disaster,
to give you a future and a hope.*

Jeremiah 29:11 NLT

Other Related Scripture(s): Psalm 33:11 NLT, Psalm 119:91 NLT, Job 5:12 NLT

He holds the plans of my future therefore, I don't have to deny the reality of what I am going through now. Everything that I am facing is a part of His plan.

He uses everything to display His glory:

When my glory is displayed through them, all Egypt will see my glory and know that I am the Lord.

Exodus 14:18 NLT

Other Related Scripture (s): Numbers 14:21 NLT, Hebrews 3:3 NLT, Psalm 8:1 NLT

He uses everything to display His glory therefore, I don't have to deny my pain because through my suffering the people around me will know that He is Lord.

The Discovery

What conditions are you denying?

___

Do you believe or know God to be a HEALER?

___

Has there ever been a time in your life that God has healed you? When? And do you believe that He can do it again?

___

The Affirmation

I AM HEALED:
I serve a God that is Healer. I don't have to deny my condition because He is more than able to heal me.

 _____

Declaration

I will not deny the pain I am experiencing because He is a healer and He has a plan and will use it all for His glory.

 _____

Memory Verse

*The Lord nurses them when they are sick
and restores them to health.*

Psalm 41:3 NLT

10
Silence

The Noise

Silence is the sound I embrace when I feel hopeless. Although, Silence can be a peaceful melody everything around me stays the same. Silence is good at disguising peace, but it keeps me from declaring what God has spoken. When I am silent, the enemy has room to push me away from the idea that God can heal me.

My dad just recently got an Echo. It is a fantastic device. I remember seeing my dad use it for the first time. He called the device by name, the device lit up, and then he made a command. The device immediately obeyed his voice. I noticed that when my dad was silent, the device didn't light up. As soon as he called the device boom, there was a light. I thought that he was the only one that could command it, but later I discovered that I had the same ability. As soon as I found out I could do the same I started speaking and commanding. What a day!!!

When I don't speak over my situation, I keep myself from experiencing the power of God's word. Staying silent means that I accept my child's sickness, my marriage falling apart, and the doctor's report. When I speak His word, things begin to change, and I get the chance to proclaim that HE IS A HEALER.

You and I can speak with boldness over our bodies because we are connected to the Creator that spoke to the atmosphere and changed everything. His words live. We have the B-I-B-L-E, so we can speak His words over our deadly situation. When we speak His words over ourselves, we can trust and know Him as Healer.

Defining the Source

Webster's dictionary defines silences as *the forbearance from speech or noise: muteness*. The doctor's report has a way of turning down the volume of our declaration. Silence is not always a bad thing, but when we allow our silence to be terrorized and bullied by our condition, that's when it becomes poison to us.

The word of the Lord says that He lives in praises of His people, Yet you are holy, enthroned on the praises of Israel.

Psalm 22:3 NLT

It is very easy for our praise to shut down when we receive bad news. Our emotions connect to the doctor's words and suddenly we stop speaking what thus said the Lord. We go silent. The coldness of the news chills our hearts and our mouths go numb. Now there is a time to sit in it, and a time to speak to it.

A time to rend, and a time to sew; a time to keep silence, and a time to speak.

Ecclesiastes 3:7 KJV:

Circle the phrase "to keep silence". In this verse this phrase translates to the Hebrew word Chashah pronounced khä·shä' meaning to hush or keep quiet-hold peace. Keep silence, be silent (be) still.

Highlight the phrase "to speak". This phrase translates to the Hebrew word Dabar pronounced dä·var' meaning to answer, appoint, command, commune, declare, destroy, give, name, rehearse, say, and think.

There is a time to be still and silent and then there is a time to get up and declare and destroy. Very often we sit in silence and allow our condition to speak to us, but we don't speak back to it. Our tongue is an instrument that we can use to speak to our condition.

Death and life are in the power of the tongue: and they that love it shall eat the fruit thereof.

Proverbs 18:21 KJV

Our words are weapons that can either make or break us. The enemy would love for us to be silent. He would love for us to stop praising God. He would love for us to bring glory to our condition. When you open your mouth, what flows from it is a reflection of the posture of your heart. We have to go before the throne so that our declaration matches our posture. Our voice is a gift that we should never take for granted.

And here's a tough point, a lot of the times we are silent because we simply don't believe what thus says the Lord. In Luke 1 we read about Zechariah. He was silenced because of his unbelief. Here goes a summary:

1. An Angel of the Lord appeared before him and he was fearful (Luke 1:11-12).

2. The Angel tells him not to be afraid (Luke 1:13).

3. The Angel tells him that his wife will give birth to a son (Luke 1:13-14).

4. The Angel begins to describe in detail John the Baptist (his son) (Luke 1:14-17).

5. He begins to question everything that he has been told (Luke 1:18).

Now we get to our main verse.

And, behold, thou shalt be dumb, and not able to speak, until the day that these things shall be performed, because thou believest not my words, which shall be fulfilled in their season.

Luke 1:20 KJV

After Zechariah was told by Gabriel the Angel that he would have a son he responded by speaking about their conditions. He was an old man and Elizabeth was not able to have children. His voice was taken away from him. He was speechless, literally. What a tragedy to be told great news only to rehearse conditions instead of praises. In this case what he decided to vocalize silenced the very thing that would free him to be AFFIRMED, his praise. Remember God lives, parks, dwells in the praises of His people (Psalm 22:3). We have a choice, we can vocalize our condition and silence our praise, or vice versa.

Why do you think Zechariah's speech was taken away from him?

_____

_____

_____

What can we learn from Zechariah?

_____

_____

_____

Here goes another verse on silence.

> *And he answered and said unto them, I tell you that, if these should hold their peace, the stones would immediately cry out.*
>
> **Luke 19:40 KJV**

Circle the phrase "hold their peace." This phrase translates to the Greek word siōpaō pronounced sē-ō-pä'-ō meaning *involuntary stillness, or inability to speak*.

If I don't open my mouth to speak life and praise, then a creation that doesn't have a mouth will do it for me. It's sad to say, but our conditions get more praise than God, the one who gave us our mouths to speak. Before starting the next section pray and ask God to help you break your silence. Don't let your current condition hinder you from getting to know Him more today.

Affirmed

The Truth that Echoes

HIS WORD IS LIVING:

For the word of God is alive and powerful. It is sharper than the sharpest two-edged sword, cutting between soul and spirit, between joint and marrow. It exposes our innermost thoughts and desires.

Hebrews 4:12 NLT

Other Related Scripture(s): Philippians 2:16 NLT, 1 Peter 1:23 NLT.

His word is living I don't have to remain silent in my pain. I can speak over my pain using His living word. He is worthy of my praise:

He alone is your God, the only one who is worthy of your praise, the one who has done these mighty miracles that you have seen with your own eyes.

Deuteronomy 10:21 NLT

Other Related Scripture(s): 2 Samuel 22:4 NLT, Psalm 145:3 NLT, 1 Chronicles 16:25 NLT

He is worthy of my praise, I refuse to be silent. When I speak praises in advance it shows Him that I trust Him for my healing. His word heals.

He sent out his word and healed them, snatching them from the door of death.

Psalm 107:20 NLT

Other Related Scripture(s): Proverbs 4:20-22 NLT, Find one more related scripture

▶ _____

His word heals, I will open my mouth up and speak it over myself. I will not remain silent.

The Discovery

What are you speaking over your conditions?

_____
_____
_____
_____
_____
_____
_____
_____

What is keeping you silent?

_____
_____
_____
_____
_____
_____
_____
_____

Do you believe that God can heal you? If so, does what you say with your mouth line up with what you believe?

_____
_____
_____
_____
_____
_____

The Affirmation

I AM HEALED:
His word is living, I don't have to remain silent in my pain. I can speak over my pain using His living word.

 _____

Declaration

I refuse to be silent because He is worthy of my praise and is more than able to heal me.

 _____

Memory Verse

But if I say I'll never mention the Lord or speak in his name, his word burns in my heart like a fire. It's like a fire in my bones! I am worn out trying to hold it in! I can't do it!

Jeremiah 20:9 NLT

11
Pride

The Noise

Pride is the close cousin to insecurity. Pride doesn't necessarily equal high self-esteem. Pride can show up in many ways. Very often when I hear the noise of Insecurity, I can hear Pride in the background telling me hello. That very hello leads me to believe that I am on this journey alone. What I usually hear is, "Well I don't want to be a burden to anyone, so I will keep walking this journey alone." Pride keeps me isolated when I should be going to the throne of grace and reaching out to my church community. Community is part of my healing process.

One night my youngest son was having a hard time breathing. He was congested. I quickly got up and went into our medicine cabinet. I got out some Vicks, I knew that the Vicks would help him to breathe. I stood over him to rub the Vicks on his chest. He starts screaming and crying "No mommy." I just wanted to help him. I knew that if he allowed me to rub the Vicks on him that he would be able to rest. Of course, his pride would not let me care for him. His pride had him tossing and turning for the rest of the night. If he would have just trusted me with his condition, he would have been able to rest.

My pride keeps me from allowing others to be a part of my journey of healing. He never meant for me to do this on my own. I can go to the throne of grace and lay every burden down at His feet. He sends people to help carry the burden of my pain. Pride keeps me from trusting entirely in God and confiding in others. The moment that I go to Him and say "I can't do this on my own, I need you to help me carry this" is when I experience healing.

When Pride says HELLO, we can silence it by understanding that we are not on this journey alone. We can exchange our weakness for His strength. HE IS SUFFICIENT. If He can hold the whole world in His hands, don't you think He can handle carrying your finances, your marriage, your children, your health, and your job? We don't have to worry about being a burden to Him. We can approach the throne boldly.

Defining the Source

This is going to be fun!!! Let's start out with the Webster's dictionary definition of Pride: *An often-unjustified feeling of being pleased with oneself or with one's situation or achievements.*

Sometimes we magnify our accomplishments to make ourselves look a certain way. Many of us struggle with asking for help because it messes up the image that we are trying to portray. So, we wrestle with the need until we are forced to ask. Proverbs 16:18 KJV is a very popular scripture when it comes to studying the word pride.

> *Pride goeth before destruction,*
> *and a haughty spirit before a fall.*

Circle the word pride. The word Pride in this verse translates to the Hebrew word Ga'own pronounced gä·ōhn' meaning *arrogance, Excellency (-lent), majesty, pomp, pride, proud, swelling.*

The root of the word Ga'own is Ga'ah pronounced gä·ä› meaning *to mount up; hence, in general, to rise, (figuratively) be majestic:— gloriously, grow up, increase, be risen, triumph.*

So, what we can gather is that Pride is taking on the feeling or attitude of someone that is exalted. We place ourselves in a higher place that doesn't necessarily align with our realities. It's hard to humble yourself when you have pride, but God has a way of putting us back into our place.

The story of King Nebuchadnezzar (Daniel 4) is a great illustration of how God humbles us:

1. Nebuchadnezzar had a dream that scared him (vs. 10 -18).

2. God gives Daniel wisdom to explain the dream (vs. 24-26).

3. Daniel gives the King advice. He tells him to stop doing wrong but the King doesn't listen (vs. 27).

4. Instead of listening Nebuchadnezzar decides to boast in his powers (vs. 28-30).

5. God takes the kingdom away from Nebuchadnezzar. And the dream he had becomes a reality (vs. 31-33).

6. Nebuchadnezzar gets his sanity back and gives God praises (vs. 34-35).

7. Nebuchadnezzar gets his Kingdom back (vs. 36).

Let's dive into the last verse:

Now I Nebuchadnezzar praise and extol and honour the King of heaven, all whose works are truth, and his ways judgment: and those that walk in pride he is able to abase.

Daniel 4:37 NJV

Was it worth losing a kingdom Nebuchadnezzar? All he had to do was listen to Daniel. **Circle the word pride.** In the verse above the word pride translate to the Hebrew word Gevah pronounced gā·vä' meaning *exaltation*.

Our pride can mute sound advice. It can also keep us from asking for help.

Underline "abase" in the verse above. The Webster's dictionary definition of "abase" is to reduce or lower, as rank, office, reputation, or estimation; humble; degrade. This word translates to the Hebrew word shĕphal pronounced shef·al' meaning *humble*.

God has a way of humbling us. He put Nebuchadnezzar back in the right place by taking away what he was prideful about.

Affirmed

Jesus Christ could have come down with a crown on His head. He could have had people serve Him but He did the very opposite.

Philippians 2:6-8 NLT

Though He was God, He did not think of equality with God as something to cling to. Instead, He gave up His divine privileges; He took the humble position of a slave and was born as a human being. When He appeared in human form, He humbled Himself in obedience to God and died a criminal's death on a cross.

The opposite of pride is humility. God has a way of bringing us to our knees. We are not sufficient we need Him. Even Paul battled with thorn in his flesh. He asked the Lord to take the thorn away. (2 Corinthians 12:7-10 NLT).

Even though I have received such wonderful revelations from God. So, to keep me from becoming proud, I was given a thorn in my flesh, a messenger from Satan to torment me and keep me from becoming proud. Three different times I begged the Lord to take it away. Each time he said, "My grace is all you need. My power works best in weakness." So now I am glad to boast about my weaknesses, so that the power of Christ can work through me. That's why I take pleasure in my weaknesses, and in the insults, hardships, persecutions, and troubles that I suffer for Christ. For when I am weak, then I am strong.

When we try to operate in our own strength there is room for our pride to creep up. We must remember that in Him we are strong. We must continually humble ourselves before the throne of grace. Philippians 2 is a great chapter to memorize for spiritual growth and to shatter the noise of pride that comes up. Pray and ask God to prepare your heart as you go onto the next section.

The Truth that Echoes

HE CARES FOR ME:
Give all your worries and cares to God, for he cares about you.

1 Peter 5:7 NLT

Other Related Scripture(s): Matthew 6:30, Find one more related scripture.

He cares for me, He doesn't want me to get bent out of shape trying to carry my burdens on my own.

HE IS MY STRENGTH:
In your strength I can crush an army;
with my God I can scale any wall.

Psalm 18:29 NLT

Other Related Scripture(s): Philippians 4:13 NLT, 1 Timothy 1:12 NLT.

He is my strength, through Him I can do all things.

HE IS NOT LEAVING ME:
So be strong and courageous! Do not be afraid and do not panic before them. For the Lord your God will personally go ahead of you. He will neither fail you nor abandon you."

Deuteronomy 3:16

Other Related Scripture(s): Deuteronomy 31:8, Isaiah 41:10

He is not leaving me, I know that I can rely on Him.

The Discovery

Below, write down the things that keep you from calling on the Lord for healing.

_____
_____
_____
_____
_____
_____
_____
_____

Why is it hard for you to surrender these things?

_____
_____
_____
_____
_____
_____
_____
_____

What are you affirming within yourself to shatter the noise of Pride?

_____
_____
_____
_____
_____

The Affirmation

I AM HEALED:
He cares for me, He doesn't want me to get bent out of shape trying to carry my burdens on my own.

 _____

Declaration

I will boldly approach His throne. He is God, the one who heals me.

▶ _____

Memory Verse

So, let us come boldly to the throne of our gracious God. There we will receive his mercy, and we will find grace to help us when we need it most.

Hebrews 4:16 NLT

12
Anger

The Noise

Anger interrupts my sleep. When I am experiencing the most pain and I can't feel Him intervening, Anger roars and alters my faith in Him. While He is in the background working I find myself angry because my journey of healing is taking longer than what I imagined. Anger keeps me from believing in His promises. I often feel as though I have gotten the short end of the stick. Why would He take so long to heal me? Is He able to heal me? When He tells me that I AM HEALED the sound of His voice is faint because I am consumed with Anger.

One night my son was experiencing a bad cough, he was in great pain. He was tossing and turning and he became pretty frustrated because he could not breathe through his nose. I knew what would bring him comfort. Everything that I could think of doing for him would take a little time before he could truly feel better. By the time I could gather all of the items that would help him, he was so angry that he would not let me touch him. I had been watching him suffer all night long and I had plan to make him feel better. His anger kept me from intervening. I desired for him to feel better, but he didn't trust the process because he was angry.

My heavenly Father sits up high above the clouds. He knows, He sees, and He cares yet I find myself allowing Anger to get the best of me. He wants to bring me comfort in my pain, but I fail to trust that He has my best interest in mind. His word tells me that I AM HEALED but it's hard for me to believe. My frustration with the way He decides to heal me gets in the way of me seeing that He is FOR me and not against me. He is a HEALER and my ANGER keeps me from having a proper perspective of His intervention plan.

He never leaves us. In our most painful moment He is standing over us, looking down on us, and acting on our behalf. We must shatter the noise of Anger with what we know to be true of His character. His character never changes. From reading the scriptures we know Him to be a healer. We can trust His healing process because He never fails. Speak over your pain. Yell over the anger and say I AM HEALED.

Defining the Source

Webster's dictionary defines anger as *a strong feeling of displeasure and usually of antagonism.* Antagonism is an *opposition of a conflicting force, tendency, or principle.*[1]

The word anger appears in 228 verses in the King James Version. Often it helps to dig and go back to discover the *law of first mention.* Let's see when the word "anger" is first mentioned in the Bible.

Until thy brother's anger turn away from thee, and he forget that which thou hast done to him: then I will send, and fetch thee from thence: why should I be deprived also of you both in one day?

Genesis 27:45 KJV

Circle anger. Anger in this verse translates to the Hebrew word 'Aph pronounced Af meaning *properly, the nose or nostril; hence, the face, and occasionally a person; also (from the rapid breathing in passion)*[2] So this is more like the physical expression of anger. However, the primitive root of Af is the Hebrew word 'Anaph pronounced ä·naf' meaning *to breathe hard, i.e. be enraged: —be angry (displeased).*[3]

Our anger can be triggered by a lot of different things. Sometimes we pray, and things don't go the way we want them to go. But our anger does not produce righteousness.

Human anger does not produce the righteousness God desires.

James 1:20 NLT

Another word for anger is wrath. *For the wrath of man worketh not the righteousness of God.*

James 1:20 KJV

---

1   Webster's Dictionary
2   Strong's Concordance H639
3   Strong's Concordance H599

Circle the word wrath above. Wrath in this verse translates to the Greek word orgē pronounced or-gā' meaning *vengeance*.[4] I love one of the definitions that the Outline of Biblical Usage to describe wrath:

Movement or agitation of the soul, impulse, desire, any violent emotion, but esp. anger.[5]

When we get angry movement happens. This movement is typically an impulse or response to what made us angry. Perhaps you're praying for a family member to be healed and it hasn't happened, so you find yourself angry at God for not intervening. In James 1:20, we see that our anger does not produce righteousness. The bigger picture is His glory. He wants to produce within us His righteousness.

But seek ye first the kingdom of God, and his righteousness; and all these things shall be added unto you.

Matthew 6:33 KJV

Anger is an impulse that we have when things don't go our way. The way we shatter anger is through seeking His face and His will for our lives. When we seek His face until we find it, and understand His will for our lives when things don't go as they should we know that He is working it all out for our good. When we use that same energy we place into being angry for His glory, we gain His perspective and produce His righteousness in our lives. For Your glory alone Lord, that's what we long for. Don't be offended by what He is doing in your life.

And blessed is he, whosoever shall not be offended in me.

Matthew 11:6 KJV

Don't be offended by something He is using to bless you. His priority is His glory. Our priority should be His glory. Spend some time in prayer before you start the next section.

---

4   Strong's Concordance G3709
5   Blueletterbible.org

The Truth that Echoes

HE HAS A PERFECT PLAN FOR ME:
"For I know the plans I have for you," says the Lord.
"They are plans for good and not for disaster, to give you a future and a hope."

Jeremiah 29:11

Other Related Scripture(s): Psalm 33:11 NLT, Psalm 40:5 NLT

He has a perfect plan for me, I can rest and know that He is at work in my life.

HE IS FOR ME:
What shall we say about such wonderful things as these?
If God is for us, who can ever be against us?

Romans 8:31 NLT

Find two other related scriptures:
▶ _____
▶ _____

He is for me, it means that He is not against me. He is not out to destroy me.

HE IS GLORIFIED IN MY SUFFERING:
Abraham never wavered in believing God's promise. In fact, his faith grew stronger, and in this he brought glory to God.

Romans 4:20 NLT

Other Related Scripture(s): 2 Corinthians 4:15 NLT, 1 Peter 4:13 NLT

He is glorified in my suffering, what I am going through has a purpose. My pain is not in vain.

The Discovery

Below, write down reasons why it's hard for you to trust His process of healing.
Example: Timing

_____
_____
_____
_____
_____

What triggers your anger?

_____
_____
_____
_____
_____
_____
_____
_____
_____

What are you affirming within yourself to shatter the noise of Anger?

_____
_____
_____
_____
_____
_____
_____
_____

The Affirmation

I AM HEALED:

He has a perfect plan for me, I can rest and know that He is at work in my life.

 _____

Declaration

I refuse to let my anger be louder than the voice of His glory. I AM HEALED.

 _____

Memory Verse

For everything comes from him and exists by his power and is intended for his glory. All glory to him forever! Amen.

Romans 11:36 NLT

AFFIRMATION 4
I am Free

13
Opinion

The Noise

Opinion is a loud sound that traps me. Opinion hypothesizes me with words that become bars. Bars turn into what I reach for to keep standing. I hold onto the bars not knowing that they are blocking my freedom. Opinion makes me believe that what is trapping me is the truth. I am so blinded that I cannot see the difference, so I surrender my soul to Opinion. But I miss the adventure to discover what it is to be FREE in Him.

As a child, I was defined by the opinions of the public school. I was labeled as a child with a "Learning Disability." All throughout elementary and middle school, I allowed the "Learning Disability" to define me. If the paperwork said I couldn't do it, I wouldn't even attempt to try. My freshman year in high school I realized that I had a choice. I wasn't stuck or trapped by the label "Learning Disability." There was indeed a way out. I discovered I knew more than what the paperwork said I understood. That year I decided to try, is the year I experienced FREEDOM.

By allowing the opinions of others to define who I am and what I will be, I put myself in a place that keeps me from enjoying what it truly means to be FREE in Him. Being FREE in Him has nothing to do with what the media thinks/says I am, what my family says/thinks I am, or what that lady at the church thinks/says I am. Being FREE in Him means that I can rest in who He says I am.

You and I are free. People will always give their opinions but your freedom in Him is greater than their words. Don't let the words of others keep you from dancing. We were created to be free. If we are prisoners to opinions how can we be free to worship or free to walk into what we are called to? Speak this over yourself today I AM FREE.

Defining the Source

Webster defines opinion as a *view, judgement or appraisal formed in the mind about a particular matter.* Many of us find ourselves stuck in the pit of someone else's mind. Let's look at the story of Job to breakdown the word "opinion." Job was a man that had everything. He did his best to live right before the Lord. He was truly blessed. In Satan's opinion Job was only faithful to God because of all the blessings He had.

Then the Lord asked Satan, "Have you noticed my servant Job? He is the finest man in all the earth. He is blameless—a man of complete integrity. He fears God and stays away from evil." Satan replied to the Lord, "Yes, but Job has good reason to fear God. You have always put a wall of protection around him and his home and his property. You have made him prosper in everything he does. Look how rich he is! But reach out and take away everything he has, and he will surely curse you to your face!

Job 1: 8-9 NLT

Satan had formed an opinion about Job. In his opinion Job would not be faithful to God if everything was taken away from him. He linked Job's relationship with the Lord with materials. In Job 1:12 God gives Satan permission to test the theory of his opinion. If you continue to read the story you will see that Satan's opinion was not accurate. God knew that Job would not curse Him, but He uses it as an opportunity to strengthen Job's faith in Him. Job lost everything, but he remained faithful to the Lord. Job hit rock bottom, but never once did he curse the Lord.

Satan's opinion was tested and proven to be wrong. Often, we allow the opinion of others to be final instead of testing it. We become slaves to powerless words spoken by people who have no idea what they are talking about. I don't know about you, but I want to be free from powerless words. I don't want to live by what someone's mind created. They can keep their creativity, I want my freedom.

We see the actual word "opinion "mentioned for the first time in Job 32. Of course, at this point of the story Job is at a very low point. His friends come to keep him company.

And Elihu the son of Barachel the Buzite answered and said, I am young, and ye are very old; wherefore I was afraid, and durst not shew you mine opinion.
Job 32:6 KJV

Circle the word opinion. This word occurs 3 times in the King James Version. All 3 references are found in Job 32. The word opinion translates to the Hebrew word Dea' pronounced dā'·ah meaning knowledge.[6] The primitive root of Dea' is the Hebrew word Yada' pronounced yä·dah meaning *(to know properly, to ascertain by seeing);* used in a great variety of senses, figuratively, literally, euphemistically and inferentially (including observation, care, recognition; and causatively, instruction, designation, punishment, etc.)[7] If we back up a couple of verses.

Then Elihu son of Barakel the Buzite, of the clan of Ram, became angry. He was angry because Job refused to admit that he had sinned, and that God was right in punishing him.
Job 32:2 NLT

Once again, an opinion formed. Elihu believes that Job's sin is the cause of his hardship. He is also the one we see in Job 32:6 that actually begins to state his opinion. He didn't like the fact that Job's friends couldn't come up with answers.

When people scratch their heads because they can't understand why we are so at peace in the midst of the hardest moments it is easy for them to come up with their own storylines about us. BUT God has already written our story. We don't have to be trapped by opinions. He wants us to be free. In order to be free, we must embrace how He sees us. Before starting the next section please pray and ask God to free your mind of the opinions that have been spoken over you.

---

6   Strong's Concordance H1843
7   Strong's Concordance H3045

The Truth that Echoes

HE IS MY FOCUS:

We do this by keeping our eyes on Jesus, the champion who initiates and perfects our faith.[a] Because of the joy[b] awaiting him, he endured the cross, disregarding its shame.

Now he is seated in the place of honor beside God's throne.

Hebrews 12:1 NLT

Other Related Scripture(s): 2 Corinthians 4:18 NLT, Colossians 3:1 NLT

He is my focus, I am free from focusing on the opinions of others. His promises never fail.

*Then Abraham waited patiently,
and he received what God had promised.*

Hebrews 6:15 NLT

Other Related Scripture(s): Hebrews 6:18 NLT, 1 Timothy 2:13 NLT

His promises never fail, I don't have to go looking for other people's opinions. I can count on His promise's way more than an opinion. He knows my future.

You can make many plans, but the Lord's purpose will prevail.

Proverbs 19:21NLT

Other Related Scripture(s): Jeremiah 29:11 NLT, Psalm 37:23 NLT

He knows my future, I don't have to live as though people's opinions defined it.

The Discovery

What opinions keep you from being completely free? Why?

Take those opinions that have been spoken over you and reflect on them. Have they been tested and proven wrong?

Opinions: Has it been tested?

What will you do the next time someone gives you their opinion?

The Affirmation

I AM FREE:
He is my focus, I am free from focusing on the opinions of others.

 _____

Declaration

Opinions are not my master. I am not a slave to what people think of me. I am free

▶ _____

Memory Verse

Obviously, I'm not trying to win the approval of people, but of God. If pleasing people were my goal, I would not be Christ's servant.

Galatians 1:10 NLT

14
Fear

The Noise

Fear barks and I jump. I run but it attacks me. I cannot run away from it. The moment I want to walk forward, Fear says " hello." I find myself unable to move. Paralyzed by the bark, I find myself frozen. Everything around me keeps moving but I feel stuck. When I allow Fear to bark over God's voice I keep myself from seeing how FREE I am in Him.

As a child I was introduced to my fear of dogs. One afternoon I was walking down the street to check the mail. While checking the mail three big dogs ran toward me. I didn't know what to do. I was scared. I couldn't walk back to the house because the dogs blocked what would have been an exit. The owner of the dogs came outside, and they ran to the owner. Years later I was taking a morning jog and I heard a dog bark. I immediately jumped. I soon realized that the dog that was barking was behind the fence, yet after I heard the bark I got back into my car and went home.

The moment I give fear permission to intimidate me with its bark I fail to comprehend the power of being FREE in HIM. In order to experience FREEDOM, I must break the chains from my past, understand that the bark behind the fence has no power over me, and run towards God's voice. My faith must be louder than the bark of my fear.

You and I don't have to be afraid we can trust in a God that silences storms and calms the waves. There is nothing more powerful than knowing that we are FREE. We rebuke every bark and place it behind a fence right now. You are FREE. Say this: I AM FREE.

Defining the Source

Fear is *defined as a distressing emotion aroused by impending danger, evil, pain, etc. whether the threat is real or imagined.* [8] Fear can paralyze us and keep us from experiencing freedom.

To illustrate the power that fear could have over us let's look at 1 Kings 19:

1. God had just answered Elijah's prayers (1 Kings 18:45) this was a great victory.
2. He gets a threat by Jezebel (1 Kings 19:2).
3. He fears for his life and flees (1 Kings 19:3).
4. He isolates himself and wants to give up (1 Kings 19:4).

So, he went from a great victory, to fear that led him to depression all because of a threat. Elijah was a prophet that was very credible. God used him to speak to the people. In 1 Kings 18 we see him interceding on the behalf of the people begging God for rain. God does it. Then the next chapter he reads a line and decides that he is in danger. The threat that Jezebel sent was in a form of a message. She didn't say it to his face. So, he allowed words on paper to lead him to fear.

Fear distorts our perspective. Fear magnifies the smallest little threat. Elijah failed to remember that the same God that sent rain was the God that protected him. When we allow the noise of fear to reign we forfeit our position of freedom. The enemy loves to use fear to keep us from being free.

Fear is not from the Lord.

For God hath not given us the spirit of fear;
but of power, and of love, and of a sound mind.

2 Timothy 1:7 KJV

Circle the word fear. The word fear in this verse translates to the Greek word Deilia pronounced dā-lē'-ä meaning *timidity*[9]. The

---
8 Dictionary.com
9 Strong's Concordance G1167

primitive root of Deilia is the Greek word Deilos pronounced dā-lo's meaning *faithless*.[10] Deilos comes from the word Deos which means *to dread*.

Go back up to the verse and **Highlight the word "power."** The word power translates to the Greek word Dynamis pronounced dü'-nä-mēs meaning *ability, abundance, meaning, and might*.[11] The primitive root of Dynamis is the Greek word Dynamai pronounced dü'-nä-mī meaning *to be able or possible: —be able, can.* [12]

He didn't give us fear but ability (power), love and self-control (sound mind). Power to speak over the things that intimidate us, love to cover, and self-control for our minds to be still when giants come running toward us. To experience freedom, we must understand what God has given us to shatter fear. Power, love, and sound mind. Before starting the next section please pray for power, love and a sound mind so that you can enjoy freedom in Him.

The Truth that Echoes

HE IS A MIGHTY GOD:

The Lord, the Mighty One, is God, and he has spoken; he has summoned all humanity from where the sun rises to where it sets.

Psalm 50:1 NLT

Other Related Scripture(s): Psalm 29:9 NLT, Psalm 66:3 NLT

He is a mighty God I have no reason to fear. He controls the winds and waves:

Jesus responded, "Why are you afraid? You have so little faith!" Then he got up and rebuked the wind and waves, and suddenly there was a great calm. The disciples were amazed. "Who is this man?" they asked. "Even the winds and waves obey him!"

Matthew 8:26-27 NLT

---

10   Strong's Concordance G1169
11   Strong's Concordance G1411
12   Strong's Concordance G1410

Affirmed

Find two other related scriptures:
- ▶ _____
- ▶ _____

He controls the winds and waves I am not afraid of anything, but I am free to enjoy and experience everything.

He protects me:

The Lord is my rock, my fortress, and my savior; my God is my rock, in whom I find protection. He is my shield, the power that saves me, and my place of safety.

Psalm 18:2 NLT

Other Related Scripture(s): Psalm 23:4 NLT, Psalm 32:7 NLT

He protects me, I am free from being afraid.

The Discovery

List your fears and the source of your fear.

Fears Source (why are you afraid?)

_____
_____
_____
_____
_____
_____
_____
_____
_____
_____

1. Take those same fears and go in the word and find the truth. Find out what God says.

   Fears: Why should you not be afraid?

   _____
   _____
   _____
   _____
   _____
   _____
   _____

2. What truth will you stand on to shatter your fear today?

   _____
   _____
   _____
   _____
   _____
   _____
   _____

Affirmed

The Affirmation

I AM FREE:
He controls the winds and waves I am not afraid of anything, but I am free to enjoy and experience everything.

▶ _____

Declaration

I am fear-less because I am free.

Matthew 11:6 KJV

▶ _____

Memory Verse

The voice of the Lord echoes above the sea. The God of glory thunders. The Lord thunders over the mighty sea.

Psalm 29:3 NLT

15
Lies

The Noise

The sound of Lies overtakes me. I hear, "You will never fulfil your purpose" "You don't have what it takes" "You don't qualify." I listen and begin to believe it. That same sound becomes the beat that my feet moves to... I continue to dance to the sound of lies and suddenly it is the only thing I listen to, my life's soundtrack. I am so caught up in the sound that I stop believing what is true, I AM FREE.

I remember watching "Super Why" with my boys. It's a pretty interesting cartoon. The cartoon characters jump into a book and by changing one word they change the conclusion of the story. There's nothing wrong with the sentence in the book, but that one word makes a difference. Without changing the sentence, we just believe whatever we read even if it is a lie. One word can make a statement true or false. I begin to think about the words that I have believed about my own life. If I were to read the pages of my life to you, we would both conclude that I am not free.

The sound of lies cannot be changed until I stop listening and replace it with truth. The truth is that God has redeemed me so that I can be free. The truth is that the lies I believe about myself have never been spoken out of God's mouth. The power in being FREE in Him is that He has already jumped into the story of my life and changed one word.

God has changed that one word for both of us. In Ephesians 2:1-3 we see that we were dead in our own sin. God jumps into our story Ephesians 2:4 and puts one word "BUT." We don't have to continue to be dead in our own sin because He is rich in mercy and He died for us. We are FREE. We don't have to yield to lies He has changed our story forever. Say this with me: I AM FREE.

Defining the Source

To make an untrue statement with intent to deceive, that is how Webster's dictionary defines a lie. We meet lies throughout our lives. Yes, people tell us lies but we love to lie to ourselves. A lie means nothing until we start believing it. What lies have you believed?

The first biblical example of a lie starts in the Garden of Eden. Satan uses God's instructions that were given to Adam to deceive Eve. Let's go to Genesis 3:

1. The serpent starts speaking to Eve (Genesis 3:1).
2. Eve tells the serpent the instruction relating to the tree (Genesis 3:2).

Genesis 3:4-5 KJV we see the first lie ever told in the Bible:

And the serpent said unto the woman, Ye shall not surely die: For God doth know that in the day ye eat thereof, then your eyes shall be opened, and ye shall be as gods, knowing good and evil.

3. Eve believes the lie and disobeys the instructions of the Lord. Not only did she believe the lie, but she convinces her husband to as well (Gen 3:6).

Lies lead to other lies, then suddenly we look up and we are tied to them. Adam and Eve fell in the trap of the enemy's lie. Adam and Eve even tried to cover it up by hiding:

And they heard the voice of the Lord God walking in the garden in the cool of the day: and Adam and his wife hid themselves from the presence of the Lord God amongst the trees of the garden.

Genesis 3:8 KJV

There's no freedom in hiding. Many of us have been hiding behind lies. There's no other way out of lies except for knowing the truth. God asked Adam a very important question (Genesis 3:11a):

"Who told you that you were naked?" the Lord God asked.

Asking this question, who told you that? Helps us get to the root of the lie.

Who told you are ugly?
Who told you are not smart?
Who told you are not good enough?
Who told you that couldn't be successful?
Who told you can't dream big?

We could be holding our own keys to the bars of lies we are locked behind. We have to capture the source of the lies we believe and put it back in its place.

The word lies occurs 51 times in the Bible in the King James version. We see from the beginning that the source of lies comes from the enemy. It all started in the Garden of Eden. The word lies is first mentioned in Judges 16:10 KJV:

And Delilah said unto Samson, Behold, thou hast mocked me, and told me lies: now tell me, I pray thee, wherewith thou mightest be bound.

Circle the word lies. This word in this verse translates to the Hebrew word Kazab pronounced kä·zäv' meaning *falsehood*; literally (untruth) or figuratively (idol): —*deceitful, false, leasing, liar, lie, lying*[13] Delilah at this point in the story is trying to deceive Samson. She is trying to get him to tell her the secret to his power. He lies to her. The crazy thing about this whole story in Judges 16 is that Samson believed that his strength was connected to his hair. His hair had nothing to do with his strength. The source of his strength was the Lord. Samson became powerless when God left him not when his hair was cut.

Sometimes we can believe the lies we hear or tell ourselves so much that we begin to wear them as accessories. We don't have to be a slave to lies, we can walk in truth. God desires for us to be free. If we allow lies to be louder than God's word we open the door to our own prison. You don't have to continue to be trapped in lies be free my friend, be free. Lies are powerless when we put them in

---

13   Strong's Concordance H3577

their place. They have no right to live our lives. They are not a part of who God has created us to be. The source of our freedom is in God's truth. We have to let His truth be louder than lies. Before starting the next section spend time in prayer and ask God to open your heart to receive the freedom He has given you.

The Truth that Echoes
HE IS TRUTH:
He testifies about what He has seen and heard, but how few believe what He tells them! Anyone who accepts His testimony can affirm that God is true.

For he is sent by God. He speaks God's words, for God gives him the Spirit without limit.

John 3:32-34 NLT

Other Related Scripture(s): John 7:28 NLT, John 14:6 NLT

He is the truth and He created me, I don't have to believe a lie. His words are true and eternal.

The very essence of your words is truth; all your just regulations will stand forever.

Psalm 119:160 NLT

Other Related Scripture(s): John 17:17 NLT, 1 Timothy 3:16 NLT, Find one more Related Scripture:

 _____

His words are true and eternal, I can speak them and be freed from lies. He knows everything.

He counts the stars and calls them all by name. How great is our Lord! His power is absolute! His understanding is beyond comprehension!

Daniel 2:22 NLT

Other Related Scripture(s): Psalm 33:13-15NLT, Find one more related scripture:

▶ _____

He knows everything, I don't have to hide behind lies.

The Discovery

List every lie that you believe (d) and the source of the lies

Lies Source (who said it?)

_____
_____
_____
_____
_____
_____
_____
_____
_____
_____
_____

Take those same lies and go in the word and find the truth. Find out what God says.

Lies: What does God say?

What truth will you stand on today?

_____
_____
_____
_____

The Affirmation

I AM FREE:
His words are true and eternal, I can speak them and be freed from lies.

 _____

Declaration

I refuse to continue to have my life choked to death by lies. I serve a God that is true, His word is everlasting, and He knows everything. He has freed me. I am free.

 _____

Memory Verse

On the other hand, I am writing a new commandment to you, which is true in Him and in you, because the darkness is passing away and the true Light is already shining.

1 John 2:8 NLT

16
Idols

The Noise

The noise of Idols overtakes me, I am in love. I dance to its beat. The sound is so addicting I don't want to hear anything else. The beat is so loud that I cannot hear His voice when He calls. It's hard to distinguish His voice when I am jamming to the beat of Idols. I remix His mix adding on the Idols beat.

One morning my sons were sitting at the table waiting for their breakfast. They were waiting patiently. While waiting I gave them some water. My oldest son had sipped all of his water down. My husband asked him for his cup, so he could refill it. My son did not want to give the cup up. My husband told him, "Son, I could give you more if you would just hand over your cup."

Idols keep me from surrendering all of me to the King of Kings and Lord of Lords. This keeps me from experiencing true freedom. When I allow the beat of my idols to be the rhythm, I dance until I miss out on giving myself away to Him and being free in Him. He could give me so much more than a nice beat, yet I'd rather keep dancing.

God has so much more He wants to give us, but first we must surrender. He is more than enough. We have no reason to hold on to the things that we think satisfy us. When we are surrendered, we can drink from His well, the well that never runs dry. We can be FREE. Let go of whatever you are holding onto and let Him be Lord of your life. He can fill you and make you whole. Turn off that beat you have been jamming to and give Him all of you. He wants it all. Declare today: I AM FREE.

Defining the Source

Webster's dictionary defines Idols as an object of extreme devotion, a representation or symbol of worship. The word idol is written 101 times in 95 verses in the King James Version.

> *Ye shall make you no idols nor graven image, neither rear you up a standing image, neither shall ye set up any image of stone in your land, to bow down unto it: for I am the LORD YOUR GOD.*

Leviticus 26:1 KJV

Circle the word Idols in the verse above. The word Idols in this verse translate to the Hebrew word 'Eliyl pronounced el·ēl' meaning *good for nothing, by analogy vain or vanity; specifically, an idol: —idol, no value, thing of nought.* [14] The primitive root of 'Eliyl is 'Al pronounced al meaning *nothing*.

Leviticus 26:1 is a very familiar verse, it is part of one of the Ten Commandments.

> *Thou shalt have no other gods before me.*

Exodus 20:3 KJV

Idols are gods. **Underline the word gods above**. The word gods translates to the Hebrew word 'Elohiym pronounced el·ō·hēm' meaning *gods in the ordinary sense; but specifically used (in the plural thus, especially with the article) of the supreme God;*[15] The primitive root of 'Elohiym is the Hebrew word 'Elowahh pronounced el·ō'·ah meaning *a deity or the Deity.*[16] The biblical outline usage defines it as a false god.

In the Bible people worshiped golden calves, statues, and lots of other things. These were false gods created by people. They look to these idols to perform miracles. Instead of looking up to God they looked to something that could not do anything for them.

---

14   Strong's Concordance H457
15   Strong's Concordance H430
16   Strong's Concordance H433

> *When the people saw how long it was taking Moses to come back down the mountain, they gathered around Aaron. "Come on," they said, "make us some gods who can lead us. We don't know what happened to this fellow Moses, who brought us here from the land of Egypt."*

Exodus 32:1 NLT

Many of us have a hard time surrendering to the Lord because we worship things that have no value. We worship things that are vain. Anything that we put in the place of God is an idol. Look at the end of Jonah's prayer.

> *As my life was slipping away, I remembered the Lord. And my earnest prayer went out to you in your holy Temple. Those who worship false gods turn their backs on all God's mercies. But I will offer sacrifices to you with songs of praise, and I will fulfill all my vows. For my salvation comes from the Lord alone."*

Jonah 2:7-9 NLT

The Truth That Echoes

HE IS LORD:
I am the Lord your God, who rescued you from the land of Egypt, the place of your slavery.

Exodus 20:2 NLT

Other Related Scripture(s): Exodus 6:7 NLT, Ezekiel 34:31 NLT
He is Lord, so I am free from worshiping idols.

HE NEVER FAILS:
Everything he does reveals his glory and majesty. His righteousness never fails.

Psalm 111:3 NLT

Other Related Scripture(s): 2 Timothy 2:13 NLT, Find one more related scripture:
▶ _____

Affirmed

He never fails, I can trust Him enough to surrender all that I am to Him, so I can be free. He won't let me fall:

He will not let you stumble;
the one who watches over you will not slumber.

Psalm 121:3 NLT

Other Related Scripture(s): Psalm 37:24 NLT, Psalm 55:22 NLT

He won't let me fall, I don't hold onto anything. I can gracefully surrender everything, so I can experience freedom.

The Discovery

1. What do you Idolize?

   _____
   _____
   _____
   _____
   _____

2. Why do you insist on keeping these idols?

   _____
   _____
   _____
   _____
   _____

3. Do you believe your life would change if you totally surrender your life to God?

   _____
   _____
   _____

4. What will you surrender today?

_____
_____
_____
_____
_____
_____

The Affirmation

I AM FREE:

He is Lord, and I am free from every idol so that He can reign in my life.

▶ _____

Declaration

I no longer desire these idols in my hand and heart. I surrender all I am for all that He is. I am free.

▶ _____

Memory Verse:

Do not put your trust in idols or make metal images of gods for yourselves. I am the Lord your God.

Leviticus 19:4 NLT

About the Author

Chrystal Castillo is a wife and mom. Outside of the home she considers herself a catalyst, someone that doesn't blend in with cultures or trends but aims to cause reactions in environments that would change the conditions of the energy, mindsets, and lifestyles of those around her. She believes the word of God is what changes everything. It is because of this belief in God that she has dedicated her time to traveling around the world and writing books to challenge and inspire others to believe He is "The Great I am." Connect with Chystal:

Website: www.chryscastillo.com
Twitter: @chrys_castillo
Instagram: @chrys_castillobooks
Facebook: @chryscastillobooks

www.ingramcontent.com/pod-product-compliance
Lightning Source LLC
Chambersburg PA
CBHW050202130526
44591CB00034B/1959